"Jon Sweeney succeeds in giving historical and literary backup to what many of us have concluded theologically: If God is presented as one who actually tortures those who do not like him, we have a God who does not 'practice what he preaches!' Without such honest scholarship as we have here, I am afraid we will continue to drive people away from the beauty, hope, and mysticism of the Judeo-Christian revelation."

—Fr. Richard Rohr, Center for Action and Contemplation

"I don't recommend a stay in hell. But I highly recommend this book on it!"

—James Martin, SJ, author, *Jesus: A Pilgrimage*

"Clear and engaging...How refreshing to read a book which recognizes that fear does not inspire morality and no one faith is given the key to paradise. In fact, it's heavenly!"

—Rabbi Sandy Eisenberg Sasso, director of religion, Butler University

"If you let Jon Sweeney be your tour guide to Hell, you'll love the journey. You'll learn a lot about what you thought was in the Bible, but isn't, and about what you thought you knew about Hell, but now need to rethink. Jon's writing is a delight on every page."

—Brian D. McLaren, author, *We Make the Road by Walking*

INVENTING HELL

DANTE, THE BIBLE, AND ETERNAL TORMENT

JON M. SWEENEY

JERICHO
BOOKS™

New York   Boston   Nashville

Unless otherwise indicated, Scripture quotations are from the New
Revised Standard Version Bible, copyright © 1989 National Council of the
Churches of Christ in the United States of America. Used by permission.
All rights reserved.

Scriptures noted The Message are taken from The Message. Copyright ©
1993, 1994, 1995, 1996, 2000, 2001, 2002. Used by permission of NavPress
Publishing Group.

Scriptures noted KJV are from the King James Version of the Holy Bible.

Quotations from Dante's *Inferno* are most often taken from the venerable
translation of Henry Wadsworth Longfellow, familiar to many and readily
available in the public domain. But for contemporary relevance and verve,
you might also check out the new "postmodern, intertextual, slightly slant
translation" of poet Mary Jo Bang, published in 2012 by Graywolf Press.[1]
It's a kick. –JMS

Jericho Books
Hachette Book Group
237 Park Avenue
New York, NY 10017
www.JerichoBooks.com

Printed in the United States of America

RRD-C

First Edition: June 2014

10 9 8 7 6 5 4 3 2 1

Jericho Books is an imprint of Hachette Book Group, Inc.
The Jericho Books name and logo are trademarks of Hachette Book Group,
Inc.

The Hachette Speakers Bureau provides a wide range of authors for speaking
events. To find out more, go to www.HachetteSpeakersBureau.com or call
(866) 376-6591.

The publisher is not responsible for websites (or their content) that are not
owned by the publisher.

Library of Congress Cataloging-in-Publication Data

Sweeney, Jon M., 1967–
    Inventing Hell : Dante, the Bible, and eternal torment / Jon M. Sweeney.
        pages cm
    Includes bibliographical references and index.
    ISBN 978-1-4555-8224-2 (paperback) — ISBN 978-1-4555-8223-5 (ebook)
1. Dante Alighieri, 1265–1321—Religion.   2. Bible—In literature.
3. Hell in literature.   I. Title.
    PQ4419.B5S94 2014
    851'.1—dc23
                                                    2013048192

To Michal, my Beatrice,
but way better, cuz
of course, she actually exists.

Contents

Contents

A Note About Capitalizing *Hell*

As Hades was to the ancient Greeks, and Gehenna to first-century residents of Jerusalem, Hell was a real place and a proper noun to medieval Christians, Dante among them. For that reason, the word, which is usually lowercased in the twenty-first century, appears throughout *Inventing Hell* with a capital *H*—until the final pages.

INVENTING
HELL

Prologue

If I had the opportunity to sip a latte with Paul of Tarsus at an outdoor café near the Roman Forum, I would take it in a heartbeat. Of all the people in the history of the world that one might wish to have a chance to meet, Paul would be near the top of my list.

It's way too hot in Rome in the summertime, so I'd meet him on a sunny afternoon in late April or May, at one of the lovely places along the Via del Colosseo right there in the *centro storico* of the ancient city. I would, of course, have to travel back in time. The year would be about 65 CE, and I'd come ready with lots of questions.

Paul would probably be in between trips. Recently back from Asia Minor perhaps, or packing an overnight bag for another visit to the Corinthians. I'd probably be a little jet-lagged and more than a little intimidated. I hear he was a pretty formidable guy who didn't like to be interrogated, and certainly not contradicted. Maybe I'd wear my black shoes; I feel more confident when I wear them. Also, from all the pictures I've seen, Paul would surely have a larger forehead, but I'd be taller. That's a confidence-booster, too.

I would begin by asking questions about his precon-version life. Did you ever attend a gladiator match in the Forum over there? Tell me about that. Did Russell Crowe portray it well? Then: Did you ever personally stone a Christian to death, or did you just watch it happen? I'd also want to ask about the whole "Road to Damascus" thing. Did you really hear God's voice? Does God even have a "voice," and if so, what in the world does it sound like? We'd be there together for a few hours, until the late afternoon sun begins to bathe the yellow and red stones of the hotels nearby. We'd start with *caffe*, then move to *caffe Americano*, and probably wrap up by splitting a cannoli with a couple of *decaffeinatos*.

When the questions turn to more specifically religious and theological topics, I imagine Paul would have quick and ready answers. You seem to have had a love-hate rela-tionship with circumcision, Paul. Can you tell me about that? What did you really mean by "To live is Christ"? He would occasionally quip, rather sardonically, *Let me also refer you to a letter I once wrote to the church in Galatia (or Ephesus, etc.), where I dealt with that subject in greater detail.*

But here's the thing: If I were to ask Saint Paul what he believes about Hell, I'll bet that he would give an unchar-acteristically vague answer. Why? For the simple reason that to the nascent Christian Church, even to Paul, Hell barely existed. All they knew from the Hebrew Bible was *Sheol*, which literally means "grave" and was believed to be the dusty deep place within the Earth itself to which every soul traveled after death, accompanying its body. And, of course, Paul lived, wrote, and was martyred for the faith before any of the Gospels were written.

There were rumblings and speculations of an after-life in the century of Christ, Philo, and Paul. These came mostly from what was then pop culture: Greek and Roman mythology, which we'll discuss in chapters to come. The rumblings then blossomed briefly in the Gospels, and then at various points throughout late antiquity and the Middle Ages, including in the revelations to the Prophet Muhammad recorded in the Qur'an and again in the writings of the greatest theologian of them all, Thomas Aquinas.

An Italian poet named Dante Alighieri changed everything with his famous *Inferno*, which he began writing in about 1306 CE. But to read the *Inferno* today is to realize how little it has to do with the Bible. There is far more Greek and Roman mythology—adapted by Dante from classics such as Hesiod's *Theogony*, Virgil's *Aeneid*, and Ovid's *Metamorphoses*—than there is scripture in Dante's nine circles of Hell. The fifth-century church father Saint Augustine referred to these writers as "poets who were called theologians, versifying of their men-made gods, or of the world's elements, or principalities and powers.... If their fables contained anything that concerned the true God, it was so intermingled with the rest that God was difficult to find."[1] But it's the Roman poet Virgil who serves as Dante's tour guide through the upside-down cathedral that is the *Inferno*. Cleverly using Virgil and lots of funky myth, Dante is the one who made eternal punishment exotic and real, as well as Christian.

Dante has influenced our thinking in ways that we rarely even notice. His vibrant, dark imagination has left its mark all over Western culture. "All hope abandon, ye who enter in," is scrawled above the door to Hell in the *Inferno*, and the sentence has subsequently been adopted by many a Goth website, heavy-metal band, T-shirt, video game, and even a few novelists.[2] One popular Finnish band, for instance, recorded an album a few years ago called *Venus Doom*, in which its nine songs are intended to represent each of the nine circles of Hell. From the lyrics, the band, called HIM, clearly wants to embrace and celebrate what feels like their inevitable damnation. The track "Bleed Well" perhaps says it all, even though it's an acoustic number.

This notion of the wicked having a raucous party in Hell is of course completely foreign to Dante, but not to some branches of Christian thought. There is the idea that those who are bound to Hell would be miserable were they to spend a day in Heaven, and as it turns out, that's inspired by Dante, too. Taking a slightly different tack, I've always found this comment about Heaven from the twentieth-century Argentinean writer Jorge Luis Borges to be marvelously suggestive: "I read a book written by an English clergyman saying that there is much sorrow in Heaven. I believe so. And I hope so. For, after all, joy is unbearable."[3]

Toward the end of the *Inferno*, Mary Jo Bang, a poet who recently created an entertaining verse translation full of contemporary literary and pop culture similes and allusions, uses "death metal vocals / With guttural growls" to express how Dante might explain the experience of entering Hell's lowest circle in a way we'd understand today. She

4

also has lines from the Rolling Stones' "You Can't Always Get What You Want" standing in for how centaurs taunt Hell's residents in canto 12.[4]

The subjects and titles of graphic novels, written mostly for young people, are also replete with references and inspirations from Hell. Glancing over the extensive collection of these books at my public library the other day, I thought how few vampires, devils, zombies, apocalyptic worlds, undead, and generally creepy and loathsome figures there might be if it weren't for Dante. Then of course Rick Riordan's gigantic best-selling Heroes of Olympus series of novels for elementary school kids recently added *The House of Hades* as book 4. Now third and fourth graders everywhere are coming home from school talking with their parents about the river Styx, Tartarus, Mars, and Aphrodite in the same way that I used to come home and tell my parents about—I don't know—*The Hardy Boys.*

Of course the gaming industry has jumped into the mix, creating *Dante's Inferno* for Xbox and PlayStation a few years ago. They reimagined Dante-the-pilgrim as a Knight Templar who has just returned from the Third Crusade in the Holy Land. He is supposed to have committed war crimes and other serious sins there, and now he must travel through all the circles of Hell in order to save the soul of Beatrice, the siren-like girl (more on her later) who inspired the real Dante, and who, in the game version of the story, is trapped there. Virgil serves as the Templar's guide, and the ultimate battle at the bottom of Hell, with a whole lot of buildup, is against Lucifer himself. The game's publisher, Electronic Arts, once hired protesters in

Los Angeles to picket their offices, shouting that this was the Antichrist, to drum up publicity.

At this very moment, tourists are flocking to Florence hotels for "Dan Brown Packages," and one-day trips for "Dan Brown Tours," during which they visit key sites in the life of Dante featured in Brown's *New York Times* number one novel *Inferno*. Literary critics are bickering with the novelist over how and where he's gotten wrong the poet and his great poem. Soon there will be another movie, and all of this will happen all over again. The psychologists among us would have a field day analyzing precisely why we seem to have such a fascination with Dante's imagination; but it is certainly due, in large part, to how the world's most dominant faith, Christianity, has embraced and preached it for centuries.

DOING ARCHAEOLOGY ON HELL MADE FAMOUS

We are not going to spend any more time exploring what has become of the Dante phenomenon. Instead, let's uncover how Hell came to be, including the role that Dante played, but most importantly by looking at everything that fed into his crazy imaginings. Think of what follows as the sort of notes Dante Alighieri might have compiled on whatever were the equivalent of late medieval index cards. Each chapter that follows, 1 through 13, fills a need for the script he writes in the *Inferno*.

Like a screenwriter might research a historical movie, Dante pulled from every source he could find. He imagined the setting, characters, emotions, and drama that he wanted to create, and then he set about fleshing it out. Each idea he discovered provided a particular insight, scene, or theme of the story he wanted to tell. That story (next chapter) was frightening, cinematic, and universal—and it wouldn't have been any of those things if he'd simply used the Bible.

We could fill multiple volumes with this sort of exploration. To avoid that, the book you are holding deliberately limits its focus to a set period of time. If our subject were the history of Hell writ large, we might begin in prehistory by looking at how ancient people like the Babylonians and Persians seemed to comprehend the afterlife, and not end until the present day with the ideas of various theologians and philosophers. But we won't do that. Our focus is narrower. We will begin with the Hebrew Bible (written from roughly 1200 to 150 BCE), which summarizes the views held by ancient Israel and is the Holy Scripture that was inherited and appropriated by Christianity beginning in the first century CE. We will wrap up promptly with the death of Dante in 1321. Now that is still about twenty-five hundred years of history and thought, so needless to say, we'll tread lightly over the tops of all these peaks, hitting only the most salient points of each!

Along the way, *Inventing Hell* will probably surprise you at times. You will encounter little-known biblical phrases such as the "witch of Endor," "shades of dead ancestors," and "the underworld." You will also see how the world of Sheol puts the popularity of certain twenty-first-century preoccupations—like zombies—in a whole new light. The author of Ecclesiastes knows how right he was by saying there's nothing new under the sun every time he looks at what's current fantasy in Hollywood and popular fiction.

Full of the mysteries of Greek mythology, philosophy, and ancient religions, *Inventing Hell* will:

- Show you that there was little agreement among Christians, before Dante, about the nature and extent of what we call Hell.
- Illuminate for you the concepts of afterlife that existed before Dante, from ancient Judaism, Virgil and Plato, the teachings of Jesus, the early church, Islam, and medieval theologians.
- Demonstrate that Dante had various medieval apocalyptic sources to help him create the elaborate architecture of Hell that most people know today.
- Shine a clearer light on the sort of Hell that Dante created.
- And reveal that Hell has nine descending circles, just like the devil has hooves and a tail.

Before we're done, you may be shocked to realize that for seven hundred years we've simply taken Dante's word for it!

It has been said that Dante's *Divine Comedy*—the complete tripartite poem, including *Hell*, *Purgatory*, and *Paradise*—contains the world, tells us about the other world, and is a world unto itself. All of that is true. People will also tell you that it isn't divine and it's not really a comedy. That's true, too. Dante himself titled the poem *Commedia*, or *The Comedy*, because it ends in paradise with happiness; it was Boccaccio who added the adjective *Divine*, perhaps sarcastically. The whole thing is like another scripture, and has functioned that way for Christians for centuries.

Hopefully, you will begin to see the many sources of this complex picture of the afterlife and how Dante's Hell is a patchwork creation. You will be better able to dissect and appreciate what a magnificent and fantastic world it creates, and why it made sense to the people of the late Middle Ages. The world of Dante's *Inferno* is revealed to be mythical not because Dante made it up. He didn't. It's mythical because it was intricately woven in the imagination of a great poet, using a variety of sources, replete with legend, upon which Western civilization once built its most basic understandings of itself.[5] With any luck, you will also find that it does not ring true in the twenty-first century.

A Quick Sprint Through the *Inferno*

Before we begin this journey of discovering what led and fed Dante's vision of Hell, it's worth exploring his understanding of that awful place for sinners via the book that made it famous. Quick is just what the doctor ordered for eternal misery, so here goes: the thumbnail nickel tour. As we go, keep in mind that there are two Dantes. There's the Dante who wrote the *Inferno*, and there's Dante-the-pilgrim, the book's subject and narrator. They are really one and the same.

Line 1 (for it is a poem, after all) opens with Dante suddenly finding himself a middle-aged man lost in the middle of a strange, dark forest. "Midway upon the journey of our life / I found myself within a forest dark, / For the straightforward pathway had been lost" (canto 1, 1–3). Let the metaphors begin! We find out later that the time is supposed to be Maundy Thursday, the year 1300 CE. But for now, he is disoriented and has lost his way.

As Dante-the-pilgrim ponders what to do next, three ravenous animals saunter by, a leopard, a lion, and a she-wolf, and he's quickly more than a bit frightened. At that moment, along comes the famous, dead, ancient Roman poet Virgil, who tells Dante that he'll show him the way out of the forest. He'll be his trusted tour guide. Virgil explains that a girl Dante knew as a youth, Beatrice, actually left Heaven for Limbo to find Virgil and ask him to help her old friend. Next, Virgil explains that the best way out of the quagmire they're in, and the surest path to seeing Heaven eventually, is to follow him through the various circles of Hell. In other words, the way out is through.

Dante agrees to follow Virgil, but hesitantly, because just as they enter Hell's gates they read inscribed above their heads a series of pronouncements, like ones etched into stone in large capital letters across a Roman archway.[1] These sound like warnings to turn back: "Through me the way among the people lost." *Why did I listen to Virgil?* the pilgrim must be anxiously wondering. And then, "All hope abandon, ye who enter in."

As he enters Hell's vestibule, Dante apparently needs time for his eyes to adjust to the lack of light, because, he tells us, he first encounters horrible sounds. He recounts screams, cries of rage, shrill wailing, even a variety of accents in speech, and then Dante himself begins to weep. He'll have to learn to keep his emotions in check. After this initial assault, as his pupils enlarge, Dante meets the first characters among Hell's unfortunate residents whom he recognizes. He sees Pope Celestine V and Pontius Pilate, who were cowardly in life, the same emotion that Dante is feeling at that very moment. He then watches as they and others like them are forced to mill around Hell's gate, never tasting its worst, and yet chased by stinging wasps for eternity.

This begs a question that perhaps you've had before: If these are merely souls in Hell—in other words, shades without bodies—how is it that they experience pain, or anything for that matter, with their corporeal senses? The answer is: They just do! You'd think that once the body is discarded, what with its five senses and live organs and tissue, what's left wouldn't feel anything. The answer to the question is Dante's and Hell's special twist: In the afterlife, every soul is a corporeal one, complete with every sensory device that the body/soul once had up above. By Hell's seventh circle, you'll even see centaurs firing arrows at shades that are trying to climb out of a river of boiling blood. Is it even possible to hit a shade with an arrow? Allow yourself to live with the imaginative contradiction. The souls in Dante's Hell are rid of their bodies, but they aren't rid of any of their ability to sense what's happening to them.

Next, Dante and Virgil cross a river into Hell itself, ferried by Charon, one of many characters from Greek and Roman mythology that will appear. Witnessing more souls in agony, Dante faints, and when he comes to, he's standing in Hell's first circle: Limbo. There he finds those who died unbaptized, as well as "virtuous pagans," people like Plato and Homer who died without knowing Christ because they lived before Christ was on Earth. For this reason, he is told that the sounds he hears are "sorrow without torment." Virgil reminds Dante that this is where he, too, resides.

Next is circle two. There they see those who were dominated by their lust in earthly life, women such as Helen of Troy, and men (even godlike men) such as Achilles. Circle three is for the gluttonous, and these souls are guarded by the notorious three-headed dog, Cerberus. One might say the gradation from Hell's second to third circles is "sin which began with mutual indulgence," lust, leading to "solitary self-indulgence," gluttony.[2] These are judgments made by Dante the writer, that the latter sin is worse than the former, and so are the punishments his to hand out. Meanwhile, Dante-the-pilgrim, the subject of his own tale, is horrified and frightened by it all.

Each remaining circle is worse than the one before it, and each is a narrower funnel toward Satan and ultimate evil at the bottom. In circle four they find the greedy; and in circle five, after crossing the famous river Styx, they see angry souls fighting one another for eternity in fiery waters, while the pouty and sullen are drowning forever. The sixth circle holds heretics, and the seventh contains those who were extremely violent in life—to others, to themselves, and toward God, through blasphemy and scorn. Flaming sand and fiery rain fall down on their heads, and a fierce minotaur guards them from leaving—which sounds bad, I realize, but it is the suffocating crowding of these hellish rooms that is the most frightening aspect of the place.

The eighth circle is where every sort of fraudulent soul is kept, including panderers, seducers, hypocrites, astrologers, and thieves. A big part of Dante's appeal when the *Inferno* was first published in Italy—and, believe me, it was a smash hit from the beginning—was the *National Enquirer* or *Daily Mail* quality of his storytelling. Sprinkled throughout thirty-four cantos are salacious tales of contemporary crimes, rumors, and innuendo. They may as well have been accompanied by bloody photographs, the poetry was so revealing and personal. The faces of many a shade are revealed by Dante to be those of people who recently, in Dante's own adult lifetime, made headlines. It is as if someone were to write a description of Hell today and place Leona Helmsley, Silvio Berlusconi, and Anna Nicole Smith in it.

By the time we reach the ninth and lowest circle of Hell, our stomachs are completely sickened by what we've seen, heard, smelled, and felt. For instance, in the penultimate canto we witness one sinner devouring the head of another, pausing to wipe his mouth on the other's hair. In another scene, we saw a shade attacked in the neck by a serpent and the shade immediately catching fire and burning to ashes, only to quickly regenerate and become himself once again. Virgil asks the shade for his name and it turns out to have been one of Dante's contemporaries.

A short while later, Dante feels a breeze in the air that seems to be inspiring the horror. He questions Virgil about it, only to be told that it's a blast from the nostrils of Satan himself—a perverse comparison to the breath of the Holy Spirit. There are many inverse relationships between God and Heaven, and Satan and Hell, throughout the *Inferno*. Nine circles of Hell, for instance, compare to nine choirs of holy angels.

At the bottom, circle nine contains the gravely treacherous. Writers of horror films, take note. This is also where Satan himself, Hell's emperor, is found. His appearance is like nothing anyone has ever seen. He has three faces, six wings (remember: Lucifer was supposed to be a "fallen angel"—more on that to follow), and he's weeping, buried waist-high in ice. In his left and right jaws are Brutus and Cassius, the two men who murdered Julius Caesar. Then, Dante and Virgil recognize the figure of Judas Iscariot, his head thrust into the dripping center jaws for eternity.

WHITHER GRACE?

Depending on your theological or denominational persuasion, you may be wondering right about now, *What about grace?* Why is it that all these souls in Dante's Hell stand outside of God's love in salvation? Being a coward or a thief or a traitor is not enough to be condemned to Hell, and if it is, may God help us all. But if you're asking such questions, don't be such a ninny!

Dante's point is this: We receive in the afterlife what we have desired in this life, and grace doesn't overcome a human nature that's unaccommodating to it. As Thomas Aquinas puts it at the beginning of the *Summa Theologica*, "Grace doesn't replace nature, but perfects it." That's Dante's perspective, too. Even more, some people come to actually desire a hellish eternity by what they have done and what they have not done; and those desires that drove them are the same ones that will continue to drive them in death as in life. It is in that light that Virgil explains to Dante-the-pilgrim in canto 3:

> *"My son," the courteous Master said to me,*
> *"All those who perish in the wrath of God*
> *Here meet together out of every land;*
>
> *And ready are they to pass o'er the river,*
> *Because celestial Justice spurs them on,*
> *So that their fear is turned into desire."*
>
> (lines 121–26)

CHAPTER ONE

In the Beginning

FROM DANTE'S INDEX CARDS...

Needed: The original human
struggle with evil

I remember the first time I saw a hummingbird. I was a high school student washing dishes at our family cabin in the Michigan woods. It was a warm summer evening. Standing beside me was a friend who was doing the drying. He quietly whispered, "Look! A hummingbird!" I paused, my hands still in the water, looking straight ahead out the window in front of me. There I saw a levitating little wonder, bobbing gently in the air, staring right back at me. "She probably likes your yellow T-shirt," my friend whispered again.

Up until that moment, I would have told you that a hummingbird had never crossed my path. In every meaningful respect, I hadn't lived in the same world as hummingbirds. I'd never seen one, so they might as well not have existed.

But then the funniest thing happened. I started seeing hummingbirds everywhere, all the time. Each day of my summer vacation, after that first evening glimpse, hummingbirds zipped by near where I was standing, whether it was while walking on the rocks by the shore, sitting reading a book on the deck of our cabin, or, again, the next evening, as I washed dishes standing in front of the kitchen window. I even heard the faint buzz of their fast-beating wings as they hovered nearby, and before they disappeared once again. I found this to be really bizarre. How amazing it was that hummingbirds suddenly populated my world! And what a coincidence—since they had been so scarce only moments earlier!

Let me suggest that our minds are not trained to see hummingbirds—that is, until they learn to see them. And in the same sort of way, all of our previous experiences, knowledge, study, training, schooling, habits, and sight lines have taught us to see certain aspects of faith in set ways. Until an actual living hummingbird zips into our view for the first time and broadens our experience and understanding.

This was what happened to me when I first read some of the texts discussed in this book. I imagine that, at first glance, they sound like the sort of "classics" you may have tried your best not to read in high school or college. Me too. In many cases, these are *just* those sorts of books. I'm talking about fat tomes like Homer's *Iliad*, Virgil's *Aeneid*, Plato's *Republic*, the Qur'an, Thomas Aquinas's *Summa*

Theologica, and the Torah—what Christians most often call the Old Testament. You probably won't find an endorsement on the back cover of any of these that reads "I couldn't put it down! Compulsively readable!" Thick and weighty, all of them, but to me, postcollege, when no one is telling me that I *have* to read them, these books have been like hummingbirds. They have enlightened me to what I hadn't known existed. They have caused me to see the world, this life, the Christian tradition that I love and grew up with, and even the afterlife, in startling new ways.

So Let's Go Back to the Beginning

Every bird, from the greatest winged creatures to the tiniest of buzzing nymphs, populated the original Garden that God created, and ultimately the story of how Hell came to be begins way back in the original paradise. But this happens only by centuries of reading into the story and adding to it. For although there was evil lurking in the trees in that otherwise ideal and perfect Garden, it was ambiguous at best. And as you will soon see, Dante's medieval idea of Hell was never really about death, but about the devil, damnation, and eternal punishment—and none of these things existed in the Garden of Eden.

A very long time ago, God created the first human being from the dust of the Earth. *Adam*, God called this creature, placing it in a lush place called *Eden*, which in Hebrew means "delight," and in Aramaic "well-watered." The ancient sages who first told this story had no idea how long Adam lived in such a state of paradise. Maybe a few days, perhaps weeks, years, or millennia. One anonymous late medieval poet wrote, "For a thousand winters he thought not so long," which beautifully captures how the first human may have experienced time and seasons. The sages also were not clear on whether *Adam* was a noun or a proper noun, for when God first creates Adam, in Genesis chapter 1, *adam* actually means humankind itself. As the first human being, adam was a sexless creature.

Then God creates Eve, a definite female, out of the rib of what is, by this point in the story (Genesis chapter 2), a definite human male named Adam. Together in the Garden they reside for a time before anything goes wrong. They may have been together "naked, and...not ashamed" (v. 25) in this well-watered mysterious place for a period longer than we have been living on Earth since their great fall.

What caused that "fall" after all? We all know the story, even if we never went to Sunday school. Was it the free will God gave to the first human beings that caused them to eat the fruit of the tree of the knowledge of good and evil, even after God had forbidden them to touch it? Or was it the presence of evil in their midst? Perhaps it was both— free will *and* evil—combined together as an essential part of their very makeup. Sages have pondered for thousands of years how creatures that God pronounced as made in God's own image could do anything other than praise him.

Then a mysterious creature walks into our story, and it isn't really evil. Imagine the rectangular frame of a cartoon strip in which Adam and Eve are lounging upon a tree, naked as the day they were formed. They are eating all of the good fruit and their bliss is evident. In the next frame of the strip, the blank face of a serpent enters from stage left. And by the third frame, this new creature is fully in the picture with the lovely couple. It is more of a trickster than any sort of devil. Its name is usually given as Satan, but that, too, is to get way ahead of ourselves. Not until the fourth century of Christianity, in the thought of Augustine of Hippo, would it become common to identify this tempting garden serpent with the larger-than-life, death-loving devil.[1]

Still, the serpent—a mythical creature full of Freudian implications—screwed everything up for the man and the woman. Without that wily beast—who in Genesis can reason, talk, and trick human beings—would sin have ever taken place? Would Adam and Eve have ever considered touching the one tree that was forbidden? We don't know. But despite its magical abilities, far beyond its species, the serpent was not a character called Satan. In the opening line of one of his most famous poems, Dylan Thomas refers to the "incarnate devil in a talking snake," a sentiment shared by most inheritors of Judeo-Christianity; but that's just not right—not then, not yet. In the Garden of Eden, evil is not the work of a single malevolent character.

There is a Hebrew word that is translated as "Satan" in the Jewish Bible, but the word is not meant as the name of a personality or person. To give this Satan too much agency would be to diminish the power of the one and only God, according to ancient Judaism. This is true outside the Garden as well. The transliteration of the Hebrew word is quite literally *ha-satan* and we see it again in Job chapter 1, when *ha-satan* convinces God to allow Job's faith to be tested. The text says that "the heavenly beings came to present themselves before the LORD, and Satan also came among them" (Job 1:6). But don't let the capitalized pronoun in our English translations fool you. This "Satan" is an *impersonal* force that's most accurately called "accuser" or "adversary."

Nevertheless, the story of the curse put upon Adam and Eve for eating the forbidden fruit has been used for millennia by human beings trying to imagine why they often desire to do what's bad, or bad for them. How did Saint Paul put it two thousand years ago? "I do not do what I want, but I do the very thing I hate" (Rom. 7:15). A puzzle, that is, even when we know better. Can we blame it on the devil? Not according to Genesis, or the Hebrew Bible, for that matter. The ancient, biblical world was one in which there were lush opportunities outside and evil inclinations within, but no Satan poking you in the ribs. Some have actually suggested that the "serpent" is a metaphor for our innate inclinations toward doing wrong and that we should interpret the text that way, as opposed to reading the tale as a literal serpent talking to two human beings.

Regardless of how you slice it, according to the story that begins every other story, we have lived amid evil either in our capacities or in what's around us since time began. According to the ancient worldview, every person had to be on guard to do what is right and to turn away from what is wrong. And as you will see in the next chapter, what they did on Earth had nothing to do with where they went after they stopped breathing.

Just as there was no personality or person named Satan in the original creation, there was also no real eternal life. In the Garden, as well as after those first inhabitants were kicked out, there was no mention of an afterlife at all. The Torah makes no mention of a life beyond death. (The written Torah, that is. The oral Torah of the Mishnah, developed in the third century CE after Judaism and Christianity parted ways, tells a different story of afterlife, judgment, and sometimes even bodily resurrection when the Messiah comes—but Dante wouldn't have known it.)[2] For millennia life after death seemed completely unnecessary. Adam, Eve, Abraham, Isaac, and Jacob are simply said to gather with "their people" after death—meaning like dust, and perhaps ghosts, in the ground.

CHAPTER TWO

The Ancient Underworld

> *Needed: The lonely, pitiful way
> the Israelites understood death*

Take another walk with me, now through the various and mysterious occasions in the Hebrew Bible when the dead are discussed after their lives are over. We will see where they go. To the underworld, that is: a place beneath the topsoil known as Sheol, pronounced "SHEE-ohl."

Sheol is a legendary place, which, like the Garden of Eden, was made real by the Bible. Our ancestors feared it as much as they idealized Eden, while we probably give neither any notice today.

Were the dead still considered to be somehow alive under the dirt in Sheol? No, that's what was so frightening about it. Is there any way to communicate with one's dead friends and ancestors once they've gone under? In ancient Israel, definitely not. Ancient Near Eastern religions practiced ancestor worship, but not Judaism. In Greek mythology, Odysseus, the hero of Homer's *Iliad* and *Odyssey*, would be the first and most famous instance of the living visiting the dead; and after Odysseus, visiting the underworld became a common theme in Greek mythology, reaching its pinnacle in the story of Hercules learning the Eleusinian mysteries of immortality before undertaking his last adventure to the underworld to capture Cerberus, the three-headed dog. But the Israelites opposed any form of necromancy or communicating with those who had died.[1] The teaching of ancient Israel was firm: Try to talk with the dead and you make yourself an enemy of God (see Deut. 18:9–13).

The first time Sheol appears in the Bible is in Genesis 37. If you remember your Sunday school, this comes in the story of Joseph, before he became second in command over all Egypt. Joseph's brothers have left him in a pit, wishing that he were dead. Then they return to their father with Joseph's famous multicolored coat, sans Joseph, as if to say, he's gone. This is what happens next:

> [Jacob] recognized it, and said, "It is my son's robe! A wild animal has devoured him; Joseph is without doubt torn to pieces." Then Jacob tore his garments, and put sackcloth on his loins, and mourned for his son many days. All his sons and all his daughters sought to comfort him; but he refused to be comforted, and said, "No, I shall go down to Sheol to my son, mourning." Thus his father bewailed him. (verses 33–35)

The son has gone to Sheol and his father wails, *Now I might as well die, too!*

It is Jacob who also utters the next instance of the word several chapters later (the Joseph story is long; some have called it the first novella in world literature), when the brothers are headed to Egypt to see the man they still don't yet realize is their brother Joseph. They are about to take Benjamin, Jacob's youngest son, with them on the journey when Jacob says, "I am the one you have bereaved of children: Joseph is no more, and Simeon is no more, and now you would take Benjamin.... If harm should come to him on the journey that you are to make, you would bring down my gray hairs with sorrow to Sheol" (Gen. 42:36, 38). Five chapters later we see the patriarch wishing yet again that he were dead, begging to be buried among his ancestors. He wanted good company for eternity. That's what Sheol was.

THE WORLDVIEW OF ANCIENT ISRAEL

HEAVEN

(residence of God above the clouds)

EARTH

(all of creation from Earth's surface to the clouds)

SHEOL

(subterranean place of the dead, in Earth's belly)

Sheol literally means "a subterranean cavern." It is what was believed to exist under the soil, where the dead make their resting place together. There they are gathered, bodies, bones, souls, and all, like shipwrecks long abandoned under water that has iced over. Trapped underground, whatever soul there is in a human being barely has an existence, making them like ghosts, or what we often call "shades."

Still, the ancient Hebrew poets were able to imagine an emotional life in Sheol. This is how King David prayed to God: "If I make my bed in [Sheol], behold, thou art there" (Ps. 139:8 KJV), imagining a place made less dreadful, perhaps even downright restful, if the Divine could be there, too. Spiritually, to be in Sheol meant to be unseen, despite David's prayer/plea for reassurance otherwise. It was a place of disembodied spirits, or dead bodies that had lost their identities, the meanings that they had on Earth.

Now, since Christians have always had a hard time waiting in their eagerness to rename Jewish ideas toward Christian purposes, Sheol erroneously became "Hell" in the earliest Christian Bibles (just as Satan was identified with the Garden serpent, and Christ was "discovered" in the Psalms). In fact, by the time of the 1611 Authorized Version of the Bible, thirty-one of the sixty-five uses of the word *Sheol* had been rendered as "Hell." The others became "Pit" or "Grave." Much earlier, the Septuagint (the pre-Christian Hebrew Bible translation into ancient Greek) almost always rendered Sheol as

"Hades"—which is similarly misleading, and we'll explore that later.

There is no belief in a future state or eternity with Sheol. When God tells Moses that he will "lie down with [his] fathers" (Deut. 31:16) in death, it is not meant as a heavenly picture. It is not even a planned burial in a place where Moses' fathers lie in state, for Moses would end up being buried in an unmarked, anonymous grave far from any of his family. God's promise was simply a reference to Sheol, where all the dead had gone and all will continue to go— like a dead letter office. It was one enormous, uniform, subterranean gathering center. Similarly, the Bible speaks of King David "[sleeping] with his ancestors" (1 Kings 2:10; also see 1 Chron. 17:11). All of these expressions simply mean that it was believed there was one place where bodies went after death.

Sheol is for everyone, whether they be wicked, godly, or somewhere in between. Sheol bears no preference and makes no judgments. Throughout the Hebrew Bible, in sixty-five references to it, Sheol is described as having fires, entangling cords, great depth, bars, power, even a belly.[2] Some of these qualities emphasize the importance of separating the living from the dead, for even the ancients knew that dead bodies would contaminate the living. It is also made crystal clear that no one can escape death—hence the cords and bars. Sheol is also described as consuming, swallowing, and silencing everyone, including the pompous, and those who make war.[3] All of this forms the essential background of Jewish ethics to this day: Your life now, in the flesh, is vitally important. Make the most of it by doing good and helping to repair the world. Death will come, and if there is anything after death, no one really has a clue. Don't even think about that. Do what is right—right now.

Anyone who has ever gone deep underground has likely experienced what it feels like to be in the silence of the Earth. When coal mining was invented in early nineteenth-century England, metaphors such as the ones mentioned above took on new meaning in the lives of many. Miners were often conscious of how they were mingling with the underworld. They discovered noxious gases, the danger of caverns, the colorlessness of everything down under, and the utterly pitiful feeling that can come with being subterranean. There were fears of going too far down, so well did most people know their Bible. They knew that Hell was in the belly of the Earth, and they were hesitant to get too close to it. D. H. Lawrence depicts the terrifying daily experience of miners in *Lady Chatterley's Lover* when he writes of "the utter, soulless ugliness" that they witness, "the stench of this sulphurous combustion of the earth's excrement," and the "utter negation of natural beauty, the utter negation of the gladness of life."

Even earlier, there were dozens of theories as to what the interior of the Earth looked like. Maps were drawn and people imagined how it might be possible to enter the Earth's interior via the poles or through some sort of occultic passage. Since the late seventeenth century, scientists have been suggesting that a hot nucleus is at the innermost core, and surrounding it are concentric hollow spheres. A theologian and pseudoscientist named Thomas Burnet wrote a book in 1681 suggesting that the Great Flood took place when the oceans filling the Earth released their waters, leaving caverns behind that would support the storied Sheol passageways. Isaac Newton seems to have held Thomas Burnet in some esteem.[4]

Sheol also doesn't tally faults or make decisions. *Sheol* is a proper noun. Sheol represents the grave. It does not represent anything any more elaborate than that. It's not an afterlife per se. The dead may remember life aboveground, various Hebrew scripture texts intriguingly offer, but they will have no access to it. This was in stark contrast to the thought and practices in almost every other ancient religion. Which is not to say that the spirit (*neshamah*) of a dead person did not roam and wander the Earth, in popular Jewish belief, after its body and soul (*ruah*) were buried in the Earth. Oral Torah offered many things that the written Torah hadn't. The Talmud discusses how the dead might be conscious of the goings-on of the living, and Jewish folklore from ancient and medieval days is full of wandering spirits. All of this persists today in many people's imaginations of what after-death is like. Witness the essayist John Berger, who is not Jewish and not necessarily speaking allegorically when he writes, "The Dead live, of course, beyond time and are ageless; yet, thanks to the constant arrival of newcomers, they are aware of what happens in history, and sometimes in general."[5]

WHAT ABOUT DEM BONES?

The book of Ezekiel tells a slightly different story by the time of the later prophets. This is a sixth-century BCE vision of the bones of the dead—those who were in the underworld—actually rising again:

> The hand of the LORD came upon me, and he brought me out by the spirit of the LORD and set me down in the middle of a valley; it was full of bones. He led me all around them; there were very many lying in the valley, and they were very dry. He said to me, "Mortal, can these bones live?" I answered, "O Lord GOD, you know." Then he said to me, "Prophesy to these bones, and say to them: O dry bones, hear the word of the LORD. Thus says the Lord GOD to these bones: I will cause breath to enter you, and you shall live. I will lay sinews on you, and will cause flesh to come upon you, and cover you with skin, and put breath in you, and you shall live; and you shall know that I am the LORD."
>
> So I prophesied as I had been commanded; and as I prophesied, suddenly there was a noise, a rattling, and the bones came together, bone to its bone. I looked, and there were sinews on them, and flesh had come upon them, and skin had covered them; but there was no breath in them. Then he said to me, "Prophesy to the breath, prophesy, mortal, and say to the breath: Thus says the Lord GOD: Come from the four winds, O breath,

and breathe upon these slain, that they may live."
I prophesied as he commanded me, and the breath
came into them, and they lived, and stood on
their feet, a vast multitude.

Then he said to me, "Mortal, these bones are
the whole house of Israel. They say, 'Our bones are
dried up, and our hope is lost; we are cut off completely.' Therefore prophesy, and say to them, Thus
says the Lord GOD: I am going to open your graves,
and bring you up from your graves, O my people;
and I will bring you back to the land of Israel. And
you shall know that I am the LORD, when I open
your graves, and bring you up from your graves, O
my people. I will put my spirit within you, and you
shall live, and I will place you on your own soil;
then you shall know that I, the LORD, have spoken
and will act," says the LORD. (37:1–14)

The Christian interpretation of this passage usually says
that it is all about Heaven, about the resurrection of the
body. The Jewish view is, although just as metaphorical as
the Christian one, quite different. The Jewish view is that
those bones coming out of their graves are referring to a
resurrection that is altogether much easier to comprehend:
a coming to life of the people Israel, in the land of Israel,
after the Babylonian captivity, when the life and spirit of
God's people will be most evident once again.

There is one more passage from the Hebrew Bible that
we have to consider. It is from the youngest book in all
of those scriptures, Daniel. Look at what it has to say will
happen one day in the future to those who have died:

At that time Michael, the great prince, the protector of your people, shall arise. There shall be a time of anguish, such as has never occurred since nations first came into existence. But at that time your people shall be delivered, everyone who is found written in the book. Many of those who sleep in the dust of the earth shall awake, some to everlasting life, and some to shame and everlasting contempt. Those who are wise shall shine like the brightness of the sky, and those who lead many to righteousness, like the stars forever and ever. (12:1–3)

"Those who sleep in the dust of the earth" is definitely a reference to Sheol. But now, suddenly, we discover that they will "awake, some to everlasting life"! And, "some to shame and everlasting contempt"!

There is a lot in Daniel that is odd and doesn't fit, and, frankly, this passage is a shining example of that. I draw attention to it in order to present all the facts, because this one, single passage from the Hebrew Bible is the exception to the rule, and yet there it is. But this vision of Daniel reflects Greek thinking much more than it does Hebrew. Daniel marks an interesting point along the way from Sheol's being turned, eventually, by Greek philosophy and Christian theology, into Hell.

CHAPTER THREE

The Awful Underworld Psalm

FROM DANTE'S INDEX CARDS...

> *Needed: A great singer-songwriter's frightening vision*

Let's not leave Sheol entirely, at least not yet. Centuries after the Torah was composed, the Psalms were written and sung. It is in Psalm 88 that we see the first sustained Hebrew vision of the afterlife, and, like many, I find very little comfort in the reference. Perhaps you've purchased Hallmark greeting cards with lovely passages from the book of Psalms on them. I doubt that they included this one. The message of Psalm 88 is frightening, to say the least.

Give this ancient poem a close look and you will see that God simply forgets those who have passed from view. Which wouldn't be so bad, if the dead weren't also conscious of it:

O LORD, God of my salvation, when, at night, I cry out in your presence, let my prayer come before you; incline your ear to my cry.

For my soul is full of troubles, and my life draws near to Sheol. I am counted among those who go down to the Pit; I am like those who have no help, like those forsaken among the dead, like the slain that lie in the grave, like those whom you remember no more, for they are cut off from your hand.

You have put me in the depths of the Pit, in the regions dark and deep.

Your wrath lies heavy upon me, and you overwhelm me with all your waves. *Selah*

You have caused my companions to shun me; you have made me a thing of horror to them. I am shut in so that I cannot escape; my eye grows dim through sorrow. Every day I call on you, O LORD; I spread out my hands to you.

Do you work wonders for the dead? Do the shades rise up to praise you? *Selah*

Is your steadfast love declared in the grave, or your faithfulness in Abaddon?

Are your wonders known in the darkness, or your saving help in the land of forgetfulness? (verses 1–12)

We see here the themes that were first introduced in the last chapter. For instance, Sheol is a place unknown, for the easily forgotten. The worries of the psalmist are that he has become like a dead person, meaning one who has gone, as all do, to this Sheol-place, to be gone and forgotten forever, even by God.

This reminds me of one of my earliest memories, when at the age of five I become conscious of the fact that my parents were mortal and one day would die. Does every kid have this sudden realization? I imagine I was not unusual. I don't remember what it was that revealed this to me, but I vividly recall lying in bed after the lights went out, my parents having said their good nights and left my room, and weeping with the understanding that I would one day be alone without them. This lasted two nights, actually, until something within me said, *Let it go. People die. Now you know.*

The Sheol experience of hopelessness is echoed in the book of Job, too, when Job cries out, "Oh that you would hide me in Sheol, that you would conceal me until your wrath is past, that you would appoint me a set time, and remember me!" (14:13). And later in Psalms another poet expresses a desire to keep on living by crying out, "The dead do not praise the LORD, nor do any that go down into silence" (115:17). Enough said.

In Psalm 88, the dead are compared to those who have been thrown into a pit, as they are elsewhere in the Hebrew Bible. Have you ever thrown something into a pit, or perhaps a garbage dump? How long did you stop and consider what you tossed in, once you'd tossed it in? Not even for a second. Gone from view, each body/soul/spirit/person passes from all memory, which is why the psalmist cries, "You have caused my companions to shun me" (Ps. 88:8). This is echoed in the book of Ecclesiastes, which, by the way, is never where you want to find an echo:

The living know that they will die, but the dead know nothing; they have no more reward, and even the memory of them is lost. Their love and their hate and their envy have already perished; never again will they have any share in all that happens under the sun.... Whatever your hand finds to do, do with your might; for there is no work or thought or knowledge or wisdom in Sheol, to which you are going. (9:5–6, 10)

In addition to being utterly forgotten in that pit, their identities become awful to look upon. Anyone who has ever read a Gothic novel, watched a scary film, been to a haunted house on Halloween, or watched *The Walking Dead* has an easy time imagining why. Once you've spent any time down in the pit, whatever comeliness you may have possessed in life is quickly lost forever, in the most awful of ways. The conjured image is what dead people look like in their coffins a few months after they've been buried. No wonder the psalmist says, "You have made me a thing of horror to them" (88:8)!

And the condition of this sort of death appears to be forever. Could "I am shut in so that I cannot escape; my eye grows dim through sorrow" (Ps. 88:8–9) sound any more like the setting of a horror film than it already does? It is reminiscent of something straight out of Edgar Allan Poe's story "Premature Burial," except that of course the Bible came first. Poe's fear of being buried alive was a part of nineteenth-century pop culture, when there were monthly newspaper reports of physicians mistakenly declaring patients dead who were still alive. One reformer in England in 1905 even conducted a study and uncovered more than 200 cases of near live burials, almost 150 cases of actual live burials, as well as 2 cases of someone awakening while in the process of being embalmed![1] So, fear of being "shut in so that I cannot escape" is as old as the Bible, but was also familiar to people not so long ago. In fact, just a year ago in Cleveland, three young women were "unearthed" alive from a basement where they'd been held captive for years—so don't think these sorts of fears are old news.

And yet, in Sheol, one's own memory and mind seem to live on after death. "Every day I call on you, O Lord; I spread out my hands to you," the psalmist speculates (88:9). That's where the minor chords in the horror sound track can be turned up especially loud. It would be far better to be unconscious in body and soul while lying as a corpse than to be trapped as a shade underground.

But wait, it gets worse. "I am like those who have no help, like those forsaken among the dead," the psalmist says (88:4–5). These were ancient days when everyone, at one time or another, had witnessed animals devouring the dead carcasses of people they knew. Defending oneself against wild animals, as well as tiny, silent microorganisms, was a constant fight in life, so imagine how "forsaken" one might imagine being after death, when your wits and limbs no longer work to help you ward off those creatures.

Then again, why would it matter? Becoming food for beasts, let alone digestive stuff for worms and maggots (both represented in Scripture), was one of the most terrifying, inevitable results of death. Dying seemed even more eternal and hopeless if one's body was to be thoroughly decomposed by millions of creatures. In the *Inferno*, Dante would feed on this fear when in his lowest circle of Hell he imagined Lucifer eternally feasting on the bodies of the greatest sinners. The medieval Christian imagination even wondered if bodily resurrection would be possible if all the parts of a body were dispersed, devoured, and digested in the stomachs of bugs and animals. That would be a lot of gathering and reassembling at the moment of Christ's return. Many medieval manuscript illuminations illustrate this, with beasts in water and on land vomiting up body parts that are floating into the sky to hopefully come together like scattered jigsaw puzzle pieces.

Then there are the shades, mentioned here (Psalm 88:10), noteworthy long before a best-selling novelist put them in his Dante-themed mystery thriller. A *shade* is a mythological figure—not exactly a "creature"—that exists somewhere between life and death. It is a shadowy ghost-like presence of one who has died. The Hebrew word translated in Psalm 88 as "shade" would be more literally rendered "shadow of death." Call it a ghost if you prefer. But if shades exist, that leads us to imagine that there aren't just bones lying down there in Sheol, but *somethings* moving around.

The most famous shade of all is probably the one from elsewhere in the Bible, conjured up by the witch of Endor in 1 Samuel 28. As the story goes, it was at the request of King Saul, well on his way to the dark side by this point in his story, that a local, obviously already renowned witch, conjured up the presence of the deceased prophet Samuel. She did so because "when Saul inquired of the LORD, the LORD did not answer him, not by dreams, or by Urim, or by prophets" (v. 6). So, Saul had asked his assistants to find him a medium, even though he'd previously driven them all out of the land (for the Torah forbids them). Then Saul disguised himself to go before her. He asked her to conjure up Samuel:

> The king said to her, "Have no fear; what do you see?" The woman said to Saul, "I see a divine being coming up out of the ground." He said to her, "What is his appearance?" She said, "An old man is coming up; he is wrapped in a robe." So Saul knew that it was Samuel, and he bowed with his face to the ground, and did obeisance. (verses 13–14)

What do you want?! Samuel basically asks Saul. And Saul proceeds to ask for some simple advice. Why has God stopped communicating with me? How can I defeat the Philistines? But he doesn't receive the answers he'd clearly hoped for. Your armies will go down, the shade of the prophet tells him.

With respect to shades, the Hebrew Bible shares something with the worldview of Greek mythology. The two were, after all, contemporaneous. Greek myth was being composed in elegant oral teachings at the same time in history when many of the Hebrew Scriptures were being written down, and the underworld fills them both. Whether it's Odysseus descending to the world below in order to ask the dead Tiresias how to make it back to Ithaca, or King Saul asking a witch to conjure a dead prophet, ancient people began to believe that death was a permanent state, but also that it was a tantalizingly conscious one.

BEYOND THE UNDERWORLD PSALM

Like every complicated book of the Bible (e.g., Deuteronomy, Isaiah, and the synoptic Gospels), multiple sources, often written at different times in history, make up the final composition of the book of Psalms. What we read today is not necessarily how it was originally written. For example, Psalm 100 may be younger than Psalm 1, and Psalm 150 may disagree with Psalm 50. If laws and sausages are two things that one never wants to see made, so, too, perhaps, is a good book of Holy Scripture. The point is, the words of the Psalms were divinely inspired, but the book was also composed by human beings.

In light of this, consider the second half of Psalm 49. It reads like this psalmist has discovered something fresh and new—that is, hope and optimism—while his fellow psalmist in Psalm 88 saw only darkness and finitude in the depths of the subterranean world. Psalm 49 begins like another passage out of Ecclesiastes: "When we look at the wise, they die; fool and dolt perish together and leave their wealth to others. Their graves are their homes forever, their dwelling places to all generations, though they named lands their own" (vv. 10–11).

In other words, everyone dies. Don't waste your time

shoring up treasures on Earth because you can't take them with you. God is no respecter of persons, and everyone goes to Sheol. It was not until the time of Jesus that Jewish groups like the Pharisees, several centuries after the psalms were written, began to believe in and teach a resurrection of the body.[2]

Other passages in the Hebrew Bible agree with this vision of darkness and finitude. Isaiah 38:16–18, for instance, makes a plea for life over death, because death is so very quiet and dark: "O Lord, by these things people live, and in all these is the life of my spirit. Oh, restore me to health and make me live!...You have held back my life from the pit of destruction, for you have cast all my sins behind your back. For Sheol cannot thank you, death cannot praise you; those who go down to the Pit cannot hope for your faithfulness." Then another prophet, Amos, tells his listeners not to look to the Lord for any sort of ultimate aid in their last days. You are just asking for trouble, he says: "Alas for you who desire the day of the LORD! Why do you want the day of the LORD? It is darkness, not light; as if someone fled from a lion, and was met by a bear; or went into the house and rested a hand against the wall, and was bitten by a snake" (Amos 5:18–19).

The songwriter in Psalm 49 continues on like this, too, using the poignant metaphor of the shepherd that we know as something entirely different in Psalm 23; but here the image is of a shepherd who is like an angel of death: "Like sheep they are appointed for Sheol; Death shall be their shepherd; straight to the grave they descend, and their form shall waste away; Sheol shall be their home" (49:14).

But then this Hebrew psalmist (possibly King David, though not confirmed) surprises us. He shocks us, in fact, in his very next breath: "But God will ransom my soul from the power of Sheol, for he will receive me" (49:15). There is suddenly a glimmer of hope—but it is not an ordinary hope; it is a miraculous one. This is a reminder that there were two figures in Jewish tradition that came earlier and whom God delivered from death. The first was Enoch (Gen. 5:22–24), about whom we know almost nothing, except that he "walked with God" and that God "took him," meaning that Enoch did not really die. The second was the prophet Elijah, who was walking and talking with his brother Elisha when suddenly "a chariot of fire and horses of fire separated the two...and Elijah ascended in a whirlwind into heaven" (2 Kings 2:11). The implication in both cases is that they were able to avoid Sheol altogether. But that didn't give anyone too much hope. There were, after all, only two.

CHAPTER FOUR

The God Hades

Needed: A colorful personality for Hell's overlord

Have you ever seen Hell ride a horse?

"I looked and there was a pale green horse! Its rider's name was Death, and Hades followed with him; they were given authority over a fourth of the earth, to kill with sword, famine, and pestilence, and by the wild animals of the earth." That's not a short paragraph from *A Game of Thrones*. It's not a speech from one of those colorful, bloodthirsty Hindu gods. It's one of the famous Four Horsemen of the Apocalypse from the book of Revelation (6:8).

Some have called it a literal picture of what will come in the future when the world as we know it comes to an end. Others call it allegory, which means that "Death" and "Hades" are supposed to refer to something else. Yet others have called it just plain odd, like Martin Luther, who wanted to kick Revelation out of the biblical canon altogether, saying that it didn't fit with the teachings of the apostles. Luther would later change his mind after witnessing a lot of tribulation and violence in the churches of his own day, saying that maybe Revelation painted a fair picture after all.

Whatever you call this famous verse from the Apocalypse, it really makes sense only when "Hades" is retained in the translation, as it is here in the New Revised Standard Version. The original Greek reads "Hades." Still, it's easy to imagine why the King James Bible and other translators chose to render *Hades* as "Hell," since Hell was a Christian concept well before the early seventeenth century when they were doing their work, and Hades was just an old Greek myth. The Bible isn't supposed to be full of myths.

Even *The Message*, which usually simplifies things so nicely, gets Revelation 6:8 wrong; it says, "Its rider was Death, and Hell was close on its heels." Perhaps Eugene Peterson thought that since Death is meant here allegorically, so is Hell, but then it all becomes a little comical. How did both guys come to ride horses? I begin to imagine next that Death and Hell, complete with black capes and scythes, will sit down and play chess on the beach with Max von Sydow, as one of them did in Ingmar Bergman's 1957 film *The Seventh Seal*.

There's really no reason why Hell should be a person, but Hades certainly once was. This chapter is Hades' story. He's the star here. For about two millennia, Hades was the god who ruled the underworld with malevolent enthusiasm. Dante made great use of this personal ruler of a vibrant playground and torture chamber at the center of the Earth as one of the myths most central to his *Inferno*.

A Sensuous Afterlife Emerges

In the furtive imaginations of the ancient Greeks, those brilliant people who brought us the shower and the sink, the map, philosophy, democracy, and a pretty good salad, came imaginative Heavens chock-full of all sorts of unpredictable gods, as well as their equally unpredictable creations. It was in that playful, polytheistic Greek imagination—hundreds of years before the birth of Christ—that gods like Hades were born and a vision of a sensuous afterlife first began to fully evolve.

Hades was once both a god and a place, and not the only god so honored. In fact, there were many who embodied both common and proper nouns, such as Earth (Gaia); Sun (Helios); and Moon (Selene). Hades emerges from the divine plethora that ultimately began with Homer. Dante wouldn't have known Homer's writings firsthand because he did not read Greek, and they weren't yet translated into Latin or Italian. Dante knew the Homeric legends as they were told and retold by numerous other writers whom he was able to read: Horace, Ovid, Virgil, and Lucan—Latin poets, all—transmitted Homer to readers of the late Middle Ages.

No one knows precisely when Homer lived, or for that matter whether or not there was really one poet by that name. But as is custom, let's assume there was and that the historian Herodotus was right when he said that the blind poet-seer of the *Iliad* and the *Odyssey* lived four centuries before him. This would put Homer's life squarely in the eighth century BCE. If this is when Homer edited and wrote his stories, pulling together, as he surely did, oral traditions that had existed for centuries ("Homer begins long before Homer," as one literary critic puts it[1]), it would mean that he was doing for mythology what the Hebrew Bible's editors and writers were doing for Holy Scripture at about the same time. Homer's subject matter, like the Bible, is the stuff of kings and courage, prophecies of glory and impending doom, gods and battles, sex and vengeance, divine favor and disaster, the fortunate and the unfortunate.

Homer's *Iliad* tells the story of the Trojan War, when Greek armies sieged the city of Troy, which is part of the Anatolian Peninsula in modern-day western Turkey. By the time Homer set this tale in writing, the Trojan War was between four hundred to five hundred years in the past. Herodotus places the conflict at about 1250 BCE; others say 1184 BCE, so you get the basic idea. The *Odyssey*, then, is the *Iliad*'s sequel. It tells the story of the Greek king and hero Odysseus at the conclusion of the Trojan War and the many marvels and challenges he encounters during his ten-year voyage home to Ithaca, an island in the Ionian Sea. It is in book 11 of the second epic that Homer first takes the reader down into the underworld. There, we meet Hades.

It is interesting that we now live in a time when there seems to be a new book every day telling someone's brief experience of the afterlife in Heaven, the glowing and sanctifying light, the feeling of peace and love wrapping around one's body—when three thousand years ago the

to see a few of these wandering shades—including a former member of his crew, and then his own mother, who tells him, "All people are like this when they are dead. The sinews no longer hold the flesh and bones together; these perish in the fierceness of consuming fire as soon as life has left the body, and the soul flits away as though it were a dream."[2]

Some shades are enduring torments at the command of particular gods—situations that seem sickly comical and dark, similar to those Dante would create later. For instance, Odysseus sees one having to repeatedly roll a great stone up a steep hill; another whose liver is being pecked incessantly; and yet another being forced to stand, submerged in water up to his chin in such a way that he's unable to take a drink to quench the thirst—all scenes that might remind a twenty-first-century reader of reports from underground CIA torture chambers. Odysseus pauses to talk with several of these unfortunates.

The first is Elpenor, a young soldier who was until quite recently under Odysseus's command, very much alive. In fact, Elpenor had been with Odysseus just a couple of days earlier as they were making preparations to travel to Hades. The young soldier got drunk, climbed up onto the roof to sleep under the stars, and then fell to his death. Odysseus and others in his retinue noticed that he seemed to be missing, but were in too much of a hurry to search for him. Elpenor's shade begs his commander to go back and find his body and give him a proper burial.

Then Odysseus meets Agamemnon, another hero of the Trojan War, who reveals how he was murdered at the hand of his wife's lover. And he sees a certain Ajax, who lost a contest to Odysseus in life and then killed himself. He stumbles across all of these and others as he takes his Hades tour. There are a select few shades who meanwhile seem to be happy down under, like Heracles, sitting at a lovely banquet among the immortal gods. All of the wandering phantoms are incorporeal, but they are able to experience with their five senses just as Dante's characters would, much later. Not long into his adventure, Odysseus has the information he needs—he got what he went down under for—and he returns to his ship all the wiser, grateful to be leaving Hades behind.

THE PERSONALITY OF THE GOD

Though Homer was the greatest of storytellers, he wasn't the one to show us Hades' personality. We don't really meet the colorful god of the underworld until another poet, Hesiod, begins to write. You've perhaps heard of Hesiod's most famous tale, "Pandora's Box," which tells of a container that holds all the evils of the world and was given to Pandora, the ancient Greeks' version of Eve, by Zeus, who instructed her never to open it. That story is told in Hesiod's *Works and Days*, and the "box" was actually meant to be a large jar, perhaps even as tall as Pandora herself. It became a box only in the early sixteenth century when Erasmus mistranslated the Greek *pithos*, or "jar," into the Latin *pyxis*, or "box." But we digress.

Hesiod was a man of more personality than Homer. At the beginning of his great *Theogony*, for instance, Hesiod recounts a time when he met the muses upon Mount Helicon while he was a simple shepherd pasturing his sheep, and the goddesses gave him a laurel staff, which he took to be a sign that he was to become a poet. Now, that's a great way to build your résumé and it is with equal playfulness that Hesiod brings the character of Hades to life in the *Theogony*—a title that comes from *theogonia*, meaning "the genealogy or birth of the gods."

Everything begins, according to Hesiod, with Chaos. As in the book of Genesis, Chaos precedes creation. Chaos is also therefore designated the first of the primordial deities. Then comes Gaia, the "broad-bosomed," benevolent goddess who births Earth out of Chaos.[3] Gaia, who is Hades' grandmother, gives birth to all that lives upon the Earth, including some fantastical creatures. *Theogony* is replete with details of how Gaia gives birth to what she doesn't even understand. She's gigantic and "painfully stuffed on the inside and groaned," so out come more unexpected creatures. Cyclops, for instance, and other things that are described as awful and frightening, that Gaia would cover up or destroy if only she could. Deep within this blend of confusion and creative energy is Hades and his playground.

Maybe we can't blame him for his evil inclinations. Hades had issues. You'd be upset, too, if your father had eaten you when you were young, and spit you up only when forced. His dad, Kronos, a leader of the Titans, devoured Hades and his brothers when they were born. Hades' mother, Rhea, wasn't pleased, and soon Hades, along with brothers Poseidon and Zeus, was forcibly regurgitated. The crew of three then joined forces to overtake Kronos and the Titans in order to take control of the universe themselves. They divide the universe among them, which is how Hades comes to rule the underworld. Zeus takes the Heavens, Poseidon the waters, and Hades goes down under.

He grows up to cut a frightening figure. Like Zeus, Hades has a long, dark, and scraggly beard. He wears a helmet, demonstrating his ready willingness for battle and fight. He's petulant and violent. Gloom dominates his visage, and he's of a gigantic stature, usually standing beside a fearsome dog, scepter in hand. Plato will later describe Hades as having hair that falls across his forehead, obscuring his face. Above all, he's unpredictable. He has a tail and uses it to beat back anyone who might try to escape his world, before, that is, he considers devouring them.

You can begin to see why Dante would have found Hades so useful, and how the Christian notion of Satan has historically derived a great deal from this Greek god.

Hades obtains a wife the old-fashioned way, abducting Persephone, while she's gathering flowers on Earth, in order to make her the goddess of the underworld. She goes on to become awful, too—a goddess who is described as majestic and formidable, a creator and destroyer, who carries out curses on men. The goddess Styx is likewise frightening and bizarre, and lives in the compound shared with Hades and Persephone, her home vaulted high up on the rocks. She is said to be the eldest daughter of Ocean, and she's feared by all of the other gods among the extended family in the House of Hades. I can just imagine their pets, the furniture, the knickknacks, like in *The Addams Family*.

In his shadowy domain, one of Hades' tools was similar

to what our generation has come to know as an "invisibility cloak." Just like Harry Potter, Hades possessed a "hat of darkness" that allowed the wearer to appear invisible. He would occasionally loan this out to friends, such as the goddess Athena and the god Perseus, who each wore it as an aid in battle, Perseus donning the hat in order to slay the wretched Medusa. Good mythical stuff always finds a way of coming around again and again!

All in all, nature and nurture combine to create a character who thrives not to simply oversee the underworld—as his brothers rule the Heavens and the oceans—but to punish those who are there. No simple caretaker, governor, or guard, Hades loves what he does. He takes pride in his work. So the Greeks transformed any value-neutral pit of the dead like Sheol into a chaotic place that's designed by a god for a god to abuse human beings at his whim.

As Dante read all of this, he would have seen the anonymity of Sheol opened wide and every imaginable, dreadful thing that came out. With Hades, Earth's underworld became the gods' plaything. Dante also saw layers to Hades that would prove useful when he came to create his nine circles. Perhaps the closest genealogical tie of all between Hades and the medieval Christian concept of Hell is the recess within Hades that the Greeks called Tartarus. It is a deep abyss, a special dungeon, and is also referred to as one of the primordial deities, together with Chaos, Earth, and Eros. In the *Iliad*, Zeus says that Tartarus is as deep in the belly of Hades as Earth is far below the Heavens. Zeus, in fact, imprisons his father, Kronos, in Tartarus, never to escape. Ovid refers to it in the *Metamorphoses* as a "yawning abyss."

The Man for the Job

Without the benefit of knowing the Satan of John Milton's *Paradise Lost* (since Milton lived and wrote three hundred years later), in which the Evil One takes on magnificent, heroic proportions of awfulness, Dante needed more to work with than the vague, often conflicting images of evil personage in the Bible. In order to be truly terrifying and seriously resident with evil, Hell needed a scary taskmaster, a brutal governor, a sadistic torturer. The biblical Satan didn't quite cut it. So the figure of Hades became his model for Hell's master.

As we've already seen in the Torah, and throughout most of the Hebrew Scriptures, there is no personality or person named Satan. *Ha-satan* is a heavenly being that is mostly an impersonal force. He, or it, acts often as an accuser, tester, and destroyer of people, most famously but not only toward the upright Job. This adversarial force is also involved behind the scenes in the murder of Egyptian children in the last of the ten plagues (Exod. 12:29), and as the strange obstacle standing in the way of the ridiculous Balaam and his talking donkey (Num. 22:22–35). In both cases, plus others in the Old Testament, this version of satan is referred to as an angel of the Lord.

Christianity changed all that with a little help from a couple of vague references toward the end of the Hebrew Bible. First, early Christians saw a smoking gun left behind at the crime scenes of the ten plagues and Balaam, whose funny donkey finds his way mysteriously blocked (see also Judg. 9:22–23; 2 Sam. 24:13–16; and 2 Chron. 18:18–22 if you're curious), never mind that God clearly permitted all of these things to be done. They began to make an indistinct satan into the figure of a person.

They were helped by a couple of scenes that appear at the tail end of the Hebrew Bible in which satan indeed seems to become Satan. You'll have to turn almost to the very last page of your Old Testament, just before Malachi. No one will blame you for never having read that far. Here is what it says, and it shocks, because no longer is this angel of the Lord doing God's bidding, but now he is actually opposing the will of God: "Then he showed me the high priest Joshua standing before the angel of the Lord, and Satan standing at his right hand to accuse him. And the Lord said to Satan, 'The LORD rebuke you, O Satan! The LORD who has chosen Jerusalem rebuke you!'" (Zech. 3:1–2).

They're clearly no longer on the same side.

Christians began to follow their noses and sensed a cover-up. They went back to two passages from the Latter Prophets and "discovered" a second fall, one besides the fall of Adam and Eve, that Jewish commentators had missed. In fact, they reimagined the history—or prehistory—of the world and imagined that this "other fall" actually happened before the Garden was ever created. In other words, before time began. They pointed to these two passages, both from the later Hebrew prophets. Isaiah 14 says, in beautiful poetry:

How you are fallen from heaven,
O Day Star, son of Dawn!
How you are cut down to the ground,
you who laid the nations low!
You said in your heart,

"I will ascend to heaven;
I will raise my throne
above the stars of God;
I will sit on the mount of assembly
on the heights of Zaphon;
I will ascend to the tops of the clouds,
I will make myself like the Most High."

(verses 12–14)

And Ezekiel 28 reads:

> Thus says the Lord GOD: You were the signet of perfection, full of wisdom and perfect in beauty. You were in Eden, the garden of God; every precious stone was your covering, carnelian, chrysolite, and moonstone, beryl, onyx, and jasper.... On the day that you were created they were prepared. With an anointed cherub as guardian I placed you; you were on the holy mountain of God; you walked among the stones of fire. You were blameless in your ways from the day that you were created, until iniquity was found in you.... You were filled with violence, and you sinned; so I cast you as a profane thing from the mountain of God, and the guardian cherub drove you out from among the stones of fire. Your heart was proud because of your beauty; you corrupted your wisdom for the sake of your splendor. I cast you to the ground. (verses 12–17)

If you turn to the expert Bible commentators today, they will explain what these passages may actually have been referring to when their authors originally wrote them. They usually explain a lot of possibilities that relate to historical events during the time in which the authors of these books were living. Rarely, if ever, do they say that these are references to the fall of an angel named Lucifer who then became Satan. There simply is too little evidence to support such a theory. But it persists.

A few passages in Revelation help the cause, most of all one that tells of a battle in Heaven that took place between the archangel Michael and a certain dragon: "War broke out in heaven; Michael and his angels fought against the dragon. The dragon and his angels fought back, but they were defeated, and there was no longer any place for them in heaven. The great dragon was thrown down, that ancient serpent, who is called the Devil and Satan, the deceiver of the whole world—he was thrown down to the earth, and his angels were thrown down with him" (Rev. 12:7–9).

Jesus himself is attributed a strange line by the author of Luke's Gospel that seems to corroborate, even though in its context it seems to come out of nowhere: "I watched Satan fall from heaven like a flash of lightning" (Luke 10:18). Then, in three of the four Gospels, we see Jesus going out into the wilderness to be tempted by the devil, and that devil is the same accuser and tempter who was trying to stand up to God in Zechariah. He has personality. So there is ultimately no need to wonder how the early Christians could have interpreted things as they did.

For Dante, this was all helpful material, because the Bible's earlier, vaguer references to *ha-satan* just didn't cut it. A great epic needs an evil opponent to match up against ultimate good. Even the tempter who became Satan, and a fallen Lucifer trapped in chains for his haughtiness, needed an upgrade. Dante most of all got that from Hades—and another statement of Jesus, this time from Revelation, supports the ancient Greek myth, for the Son of Man says to the author of the Apocalypse: "I am alive forever and ever; and I have the keys of Death and of Hades" (Rev. 1:18).

WHAT MYTH DOES

Why would Jesus say such a thing—"I have the keys of Hades"—if it weren't true? Did he literally believe the Greek myth of Hades as a place, as a god? Of course not. To even pose the question is to misunderstand how myth works. The philosopher George Santayana once said, "Truth is only believed when someone has invented it well," which helps to explain why great myths and stories hold such power.

Maybe we should ask if the ancient Greeks really believed all the stuff their poets said and wrote about the creation of the world, gods and goddesses, who ruled the underworld, and all of that. Did they? The answer is no and yes. No, because *credo* was not in their vocabulary. They were not a people, like we tend to be, who used belief as their primary way of entering the world. For us, raised in the shadow of the Enlightenment, belief is premeditated, articulated, a primary way of defining ourselves. For the last few hundred years at least, we've been a people who almost literally wear our beliefs on our sleeves for all to see, and we've deliberately congregated and separated ourselves based upon beliefs. This is beginning to change, even for Christians, and we're beginning to discover that faithfulness is possible with a new type of agnosticism, the kind that simply ceases to believe in belief.[4]

For ancient people, "I believe" was always less common; "I am" was more their style. The story your people told of who you are—where you've come from, who you belong to—was far more important than what you said you believed. That is why the account of creation in *Theogony* and the myth-making powers of Homer were so powerful. Ancient people did not so much align their beliefs around myths as they pledged their allegiance to an identity created by them. For this reason, the world's noble warrior-king, Alexander the Great (d. 323 BCE), kept a copy of Homer's *Iliad* with him while he galloped around the globe conquering the known world. Alexander's heroics were aimed at reclaiming the mantle of Achilles; that's who he wanted to be. Christians would later read and remember the lives of the saints in much the same way: by imitating them.

A myth was a picture of reality, and to them the picture was much stronger than words. Yes, they believed it. So our best response might be simply to try to enter into the world as they saw it. Peter Barnes, one of my favorite playwrights, once explained, "History is not history unless it is imagined. No one I know was present in the distant past, so the past, like the future, is an act of imagination."[5]

CHAPTER FIVE

Virgil and the Myth of Empire

FROM DANTE'S INDEX CARDS...

> *Needed: Evidence of God's*
> *imperial intentions for*
> *Rome and Christianity*

You already know that Dante's tour guide through Hell is a dead Roman poet. Perhaps you've realized that is more than a little odd.

Dante has not chosen a respected medieval pope like Saint Gregory the Great, or a pivotal figure from the Bible like Moses or Saint Peter, to escort him knowledgeably through the afterlife. He didn't select an honored saint like the Virgin Mary, queen of them all; or Francis of Assisi, so recently blessed that all Italians felt like he'd only just left, as his tour guide. He didn't even pick Jesus Christ himself. No, Dante has selected a dead poet—Virgil, author of the *Aeneid*. How strange.

Virgil lived a generation before the time of Jesus, making him by default what we often call a "pagan." The word originated in the late Middle Ages to mean native people who may observe some sort of spiritual tradition but who live entirely apart from one of the world's major religions. Christians used to speak of such people as those who had never been exposed to the "light of Christ." As Saint Cyprian expressed it in the third century, "extra Ecclesiam nulla salus" (there is no salvation outside the church).

Experts have written volumes to speculate why Dante chose this particular historical/literary figure to guide his pilgrim through Hell's circles and caverns. Saint Augustine had famously confessed his love for reading pagan writers like Virgil in his *Confessions*. He said that he put poets and rhetoric away like childish things (which actually meant that he'd internalized and Christianized them thoroughly). The point is, Augustine had confessed it as sin. Not so, Dante. He calls Virgil "my master." He chose a pagan for the starring role.

One reason, surely, why Dante has Virgil showing him around is that he viewed himself as one of the great poets, and so only another great could show him the way. There were no great Christian poets to choose from before Dante. And narratively, using Virgil as his guide through the *Inferno* was a helpful device because Virgil had supposedly been there before. As Virgil tells Dante-the-pilgrim:

> *Thou follow me, and I will be thy guide,*
> *And lead thee hence through the eternal place,*
> *Where thou shalt hear the desperate lamentations,*

Shalt see the ancient spirits disconsolate,
Who cry out each one for the second death.
(1.113–17)

He'd been there because he, too, had written about the underworld, but also, of course, because he was dead!

Dante also revered Virgil because he believed the myth Virgil created some thirteen hundred years before Dante was born. I'm referring to the "Myth of Empire"—the notion that the city of Rome, the Roman Empire, its emperors, and by extension Christianity itself, were all created by divine ordination. It wasn't unusual for Dante to believe the Roman Empire was God's favored way of governing the world; every proud Roman of the Middle Ages did. They also thought that when the empire crumbled in the fifth century, evil had won, but only temporarily, for God would surely make Rome (and with it, Christianity) rise once again. This was mostly because of Virgil.

WHO VIRGIL WAS

Unlike some famous earlier poets, there is little doubt that Virgil was a real person who actually existed. He was born Publius Vergilius Maro, probably of Gaulish or Umbrian descent. He lived from 70 to 19 BCE and came from a family that likely owned land, given that he was obviously a well-educated boy. He attended schools in Naples and Rome, studying rhetoric before turning to poetry.

Virgil knew his Homer and Ovid and all of Latin literature backward and forward and seems to have emerged into adulthood ready to take on the mantle of "Rome's poet." He wrote two major books before turning to the *Aeneid*, which became his life's work, though it was never actually published during his lifetime. In fact, Virgil left instructions that *Aeneid* should be destroyed upon his death, and it took Augustus himself, the founding emperor of the Roman Empire, who reigned from 27 to 14 BCE, to personally intervene and order the manuscript to be published without delay. Then they buried Virgil in Naples with honor.

In ancient days a poet was a seer, an oracle, almost like a priest. He was regarded as a man with deep spiritual insight—not simply a verse-maker. His lyricism was intrinsically connected to his wisdom—the first couldn't be separated from the second in the imaginations of ancient people. No one ever read a poem and remarked how lovely it was. Poems weren't judged in that way. A poet's ideas were thought to originate outside of himself, from the divine muse. This is why, in the ancient and medieval eras, it was common for a spiritual seeker to open a book of great poetry and point his finger to a line at random. That line, he believed, would speak some sort of truth to his soul. Saint Augustine tells us about this in the *Confessions*.[1] In other words, to be a poet was a highly respected and exclusive role to play in society. We can hardly imagine this today, when poetry often feels ordinary and ubiquitous and we no longer seem to know how to judge what is special and what is not. Anyone can write a poem today. That did not used to be true, or at least ancient people knew that only a very select few could truly be "poets."

Ancient poetry actually predates literacy. Human beings composed songs, myths, and legends in verse centuries, perhaps even millennia, before they could read and write their own names. Poets were a society's historians. They were the ones who were charged with remembering a people's laws and customs, as well as the origins of life itself. This is why Homer and Virgil wrote epic poems: because they had such big stories to tell! They weren't composing poems about themselves, but about their people and the world writ large.

THE MYTH VIRGIL CREATED

Virgil picks up where Homer left off. Homer is to Virgil as the Torah is to the Prophets and as the Hebrew Bible is to the New Testament; the first is the foundation for the second, and the second wouldn't make much sense without the first. Two thousand years ago, Roman schoolchildren were learning their Homer just as Jewish children were memorizing their Torah. In Dante's day, the schoolkids were also memorizing their *Aeneid*.

The story of the *Aeneid* revolves around the person and character of Aeneas, a relatively minor character from the *Iliad*. Aeneas is the son of a prince (Anchises) and a goddess (Aphrodite in Greek, or Venus in Roman, mythology) who survived the Trojan Wars because gods like Aphrodite and Poseidon were frequently saving his life, as it was often said, for some unknown future destiny.

You should imagine Aeneas looking a lot like Moses. Every sculpture or relief of him depicts a tall man with a well-defined upper body, displaying his muscular chest open-toga, a strong chin, and a full, manly beard. Downright godlike! As for his character, Virgil portrays Aeneas as constantly pious, prayerful, and grateful, qualities that T. S. Eliot thought made him "the antithesis, in important respects, of either Achilles or Odysseus," and "an analogue and foreshadow of Christian humility."[2] That's the same Eliot who was a champion of the "Christian Europe" that prevailed for nearly two thousand years, and he praised Virgil for its origins. Hence the saintlike portrait. But many of us now know that, tied up with empire as it was, there was little truly Christian about those two millennia except for how power was handed down, the music, the architecture, and the poetry. But I'm getting ahead of myself.

The *Aeneid* begins at the end of the battles at Troy, at a time that we have already presumed, based on Herodotus's estimation, to have been about 1250 BCE. The setting is the eastern Mediterranean Sea, as the ships of Troy flee a burning city toward the shores of Italy. They have a distance to travel by sea that is about three times that traveled by Moses and the Hebrews from Egypt to Palestine. Aeneas is the leader of the fleeing remnant, and it has been foretold that he'll land in a place where a new civilization will be founded. A noble and courageous people will form who will become essential for governing every part of the known world. If bells of similarity are ringing in your head, they should. There's an echo of the Exodus in this, also of Christianity growing out of Judaism, the Pilgrims fleeing for a holier life in America, and even Joseph Smith discovering tablets of gold in upstate New York. Most of our grand stories of the births of religions and empires begin as offshoots of some earlier, mighty tradition.

Many locations throughout the Mediterranean are visited by Aeneas's fleet of ships and considered as possible locations for this blessed city to be born, but none are quite right. They travel from the west coast of Turkey to Crete, then around the horn of Italy, past Carthage (today's Tunis) at the northeast tip of Africa, to Sicily and then beyond. The ancient Greek Empire had never extended to the west past Sicily, but Aeneas would. Beyond the Bay of Naples, fifteen miles inland from where the Tiber River flows into the Tyrrhenian Sea, in a place deemed holy where seven hills come together, the "Eternal City" of Rome is founded, a suitable replacement for the divine Troy.

Along the way many fallen comrades from the Trojan Wars are lamented and praised. Aeneas and his comrades fight many battles in each place, some violently, and some of the personal and emotional sort, such as when Aeneas has to contend with his own mother, Venus, who at times wants to thwart his plans; and when Aeneas is tricked into having sex with Dido, who wants to marry him and settle down in Carthage, keeping him away from his final destination. After spending a night together, Aeneas spurns her and Dido commits suicide, leaving behind a note that "foretells" the great conflict that would occur between

Rome and Carthage, culminating with Hannibal's reign in Carthage in about 200 BCE. Virgil was, after all, a poet, poets explained history, and history was understood as the past but also lived into the future.

Aeneas's Visit to Hades

Along the way, Virgil depicts Aeneas following in Odysseus's footsteps by visiting the underworld, just as the earlier hero had done in Homer's *Odyssey*. Hades is pictured as a gorge, a "ghostly realm" where "Grief and the pangs of Conscience make their beds."[3] What Aeneas sees first down there are things we commonly see, even now, aboveground when death is approaching: poverty, old age, disease, war, and conflict. Then he glimpses a broad elm tree that offers shade in the form of what he calls faded dreams and monsters. The monsters are creatures such as centaurs, gorgons, and Cerberus, the three-throated hound, all poised to torture unhappy souls.

Above all, with a famous simile, Virgil sees throngs of the dead along the shores of the river Styx, "as thick as leaves in autumn woods at the first frost," referring to the vast numbers of those pleading for a turn to cross into Hades and find peace in burial once and for all.[4] Some, we are told, will wait one hundred years until it is their turn. The dead are most helpless, you see, as they wander, phantomlike, before finding a resting place. Their pleading for a place on the ferry is nothing like hoping for Heaven; it does not communicate a threat of Hell, either, for they are actually desiring to get in. This is still something that's clearly in between.

ROME'S FOUNDING REVEALED

It is right there in the underworld, in book 6 of the *Aeneid*, where Aeneas talks with the shade of his dead father, Anchises, and father tells son how the great city of Rome is to be founded: by Aeneas's descendant-to-be, Romulus. Romulus and his twin brother, Remus, will be born to a vestal virgin raped by Mars, the god of war. The twins will be abandoned along the bank of the Tiber to die, after their mother herself dies in childbirth. If you've ever visited Italy, you've probably seen on coins, sculpture, and T-shirts the city of Rome's famous emblem of a she-wolf suckling two young boys. Those boys are meant to be Romulus and Remus, who as disregarded orphans find the wolf's nourishing milk with a tenacity that will become a lasting mark of the Roman character.

As they grow, Romulus and Remus eventually fight over the best location for the great city and Romulus murders his brother. You'd think that, à la Cain and Abel, Remus would then go down in history as the sanctified one, but he doesn't. As one contemporary writer puts it, "If things had gone differently and Remus had [founded the city], we might now talk about visiting Reem [instead of Roma]."[5] The Romans revered Romulus. The ancient historian Plutarch says that after burying his brother, Romulus "set to building his city" and did it in accordance with ancient Tuscan religious rituals. He also compares Theseus, the equally mythical founding hero of ancient Athens, to Romulus and finds Romulus and the founding of Rome to be more historically accurate. Of course, Plutarch was a proud Roman.

Longstanding tradition places the birth of the twins in 771, and the city's birth at 753—both BCE. Every citizen of ancient Rome grew up counting the history of the world from that year forward. So Christ was born in the Roman year 753.

Through all of this divinely assisted travel and suckling, the Trojans are ready to become the people who settle the new Eternal City, as well as the race of hardy men and women who are to thank for building all that would become (already in Virgil's own lifetime) the Roman Empire. If we were beginning to see parallels to the birth of other religions and empires earlier, now we hear even louder echoes of God making a promise to Abram. That blessed civilization, Anchises tells Aeneas, will eventually be ruled by Caesar Augustus, and from it the whole world. "All who shall one day pass under the dome / Of the great sky...," Virgil says, will be saved from harm.[6]

These elaborate legends were supposed to explain why and how Rome had become so adept at empire-building. Whereas the Greeks had valued discovery and beauty, the Romans valued power and consolidation. E. H. Gombrich summarizes this well: "They were not as quick-thinking or as inventive as the Athenians....Nor was reflecting on the world and on life so vital to them....Their homes... and their land—these were what mattered....They loved their native city and its soil and would do anything and everything to increase its prosperity and power."[7] And they treasured their heritage as God's new chosen people.

The Christian Church would be born into this Rome and this empire when Constantine I defeated Maxentius at the Battle of the Milvian Bridge in 312 CE, crediting the God of Christianity for his victory and making Christianity the faith of the Western world. Many books have been written—especially in recent years as emergence Christians come to terms with Christianity's imperial past—to envision a faith that is comfortable without this sort of power, rather than a faith that seeks it. That's what Christians did as soon as it was feasible, beginning in 312, spreading rapidly on Rome's well-constructed roads, finding avenues of influence at every level of government, making Christianity the religion of the empire by sword or by spirit. As the empire conquered more lands and people, Christianity marched in behind them, and even after Rome's collapse, Christianity expected and demanded the hegemony that they believed was theirs by divine right.

HOW DANTE USED THE ROMAN MYTH

Did Aeneas really wake from a dream in which he learned that his beloved Troy was in flames and resolve to lead a righteous remnant of survivors on an epic journey to discover a new "holy" city? Of course not. Did Aeneas really battle with gods and give birth to a great civilization? Of course not. All of this happened just like Athena, the goddess of wisdom and warfare, was born fully armed straight out of Zeus's forehead. But it might as well have all happened that way, so important was the myth for forming the Roman Empire.

Never mind if it was true as we may understand truth.

Ancient and medieval Romans believed the tale of Aeneas, which means that they interpreted their lives through the story told in Virgil's myth. The emperor Augustus had excellent reasons for *wanting* it to be true, and the average Roman knew nothing else. A myth was true if it had the power to bind people together, if they were drawn to it, if it captivated, if it said something true about their lives and who they wanted to be; and Virgil's creation did all of those things. This is why even Socrates was able to say to Callicles in the dialogue known as *Gorgias*: "Listen, then, as story-tellers say, to a very pretty tale, which I dare say that you may be disposed to regard as a fable only, but which, as I believe, is a true tale, for I mean to speak the truth."[8]

Dante had his own reasons for wanting the myth of Aeneas and the birth of Roman civilization to be true. He was one of Rome's proudest descendants. The connection between Dante's Florence and the city of Rome was an intimate one, and all Florentines believed Rome was their mother; and most families, including Dante's, claimed a line of descent from a famous Roman ancestor. Dante was also writing the *Inferno* in the first decade of the fourteenth century, and Italy hadn't had a resident emperor since Frederick II died in 1250. He wasn't alone in his concern about this. A land with a great, even divinely ordained, founding deserved to rule itself.

So, for all of these reasons, the story told in the *Aeneid* was as true as true could be in the mind of Dante as well as in the minds of Roman citizens for close to two thousand years. It was a myth of the self-defining kind and quickly became the national epic of the Roman Empire. The *Aeneid*

CHAPTER SIX

When the Soul Went Immortal

FROM DANTE'S INDEX CARDS . . .

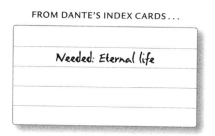

Needed: Eternal life

A man walks into a bar in Sheol. Dark and dusty, there's hardly enough light by which to see. But he really wants a glass of whiskey, so he yells, "Is there a bartender in the house?!" A long silence follows. Finally, the man sees a faint ghost appearing as a reflection in the bar glass. "Hey, what does it take for a guy to get a drink around here?!" he calls out. The reflection promptly disappears. Then there's another long silence, followed by another shade passing by, this one less distinct than the last. The thirsty man finally hops over the bar, and promptly dies. It turns out that he'd been dreaming, and now he, too, is in Sheol.

That's about all Dante would have had as material for Hell had he only the Hebrew Bible to work from. There existed a lonely, quiet underworld where people went after death and their shades wandered forever. Boring. Then came the Greeks.

We almost can't plumb ancient Greek thought enough if we want to get to the bottom of what Dante used to create his *Inferno*. In this chapter, we look briefly at their most important idea of all—and it comes from Socrates and Plato. (Socrates said it; Plato wrote it down. That's how it always worked between them.) Here, finally, the soul is ready to take on an identity of its own. First, it is separated from the body at death. Second, it is fully conscious and alive after the body is dead and gone. And third, like a platinum album, the soul goes immortal.

Why does this matter? Because a soul that's distinct from the body and possessed of consciousness for eternity makes a vibrant afterlife possible. Simply put, the purpose and use of Hell in Christianity would fall apart without the immortality of the soul. And with the old paradigm of cosmic theism being replaced over the last century by new understandings of God as a personal guiding force in a heart and soul, this appears to be one of the most enduring religious ideas of all time. You're in good company if you thought it originated with the Bible, but you'd be wrong.

How the Soul Went Immortal

Homer's *Odyssey* had shown shades of people retaining their identity after death, but they were still trapped in the underworld, so consciousness was as much a curse as it was a blessing. This is what caused Achilles to say to Odysseus,

"Say not a word...in death's favor; I would rather be a paid servant in a poor man's house and be above ground than king of kings among the dead."[1] But hundreds of years after Homer, Socrates seems at times genuinely unafraid of Sheol or Hades, of vanishing from sight forever, believing that there will be some real continuity from this life to the next, something beyond a trapped existence underground.

Throughout Plato's dialogues, Socrates dispenses a variety of opinions about the afterlife. In the *Apologia*, he speaks as if death will be a quiet sleep, sounding a lot like Sheol. At other times he seems to say that no one knows anything for certain about what will come. At still other times he talks as if the Hades of Homer is the be-all and end-all. And at least once, Socrates reflects that death will bring with it good occasions to sit and chat with the greatest minds of past ages. Ah, now we're on to something.

In one of the most important dialogues Plato ever recorded, we see Socrates in conversation with a group of students and friends on the day before his execution. The Athenian courts have sentenced him to death because of his religious beliefs. They convicted him of a capital crime: questioning the godly pantheon, making him a traitor, which was similar and yet different from what Christians would later call a heretic. The dialogue is called *Phaedo*. The conversation takes place in an Athenian prison and centers entirely around beliefs in the afterlife.

Socrates' closest friends are there and death hangs in the air. They all know that their teacher is soon to drink hemlock. A young disciple, Cebes, begins by asking Socrates about the value of death versus life. In no uncertain terms,

Socrates tells Cebes that he is looking forward to death, because then his soul will separate from his body, which only plagues him with temptations and unhealthy diversions. This makes another disciple, Simmias, laugh. To live a life without bodily pleasure is like being already dead, he says. Perhaps, Socrates replies, but if the soul is to apprehend love, wisdom, and justice, it can ultimately do that only when it is rid of a human body. "The soul in herself must behold all things in themselves," he explains.[2]

Then Simmias and Cebes have more questions. Is it true, as some say, that the human soul wanders, or is simply extinguished, upon death? they ask. Other interlocutors offer alternate possibilities. For example, perhaps each soul may be the possession of a particular body, and so when the journey of one is done so is the other. But Socrates sets out to correct them all.

"The soul is in the very likeness of the divine," he says, "immortal, intelligible, uniform, indissoluble, and unchangeable."[3] Then he explains how a soul is essentially separate from the body it inhabits. Souls give life to human bodies. Christian theologians would later use this distinction to explain that angels don't have souls, because they aren't embodied.[4]

Socrates distinguishes a soul that is pure when the body dies from a soul that is impure. The first will have "no bodily taint" and will "depart to the invisible world— to the divine and immortal...arriving...in bliss and... released from the error and folly of humankind, their fears and wild passions...and forever dwells...in company with the gods." In contrast, the second "has been polluted, is impure at the time of her departure, is the companion and

76

servant of the body always, is in love with and fascinated by the body and by the desires and pleasures of the body, until she is led to believe that the truth only exists in bodily form, which a person may touch, see, taste, and use for the purposes of his lusts." Either way, the soul is something altogether distinct from the corporeality of the body.

This is suddenly a 4.0 version of spiritual anthropology, radically different from what Socrates and his students would have been exposed to as children in ancient Greece. It was similar to Galileo's discovery that the Earth revolves around the sun. Suddenly, the Earth was no longer understood to be a stationary object, but a changing one, and not the center of the universe, but only one point in it. Or, it is like in 1869 when a Swiss physician named Friedrich Miescher looked closely at the bodily fluid on a discarded surgical bandage and began to figure out that it contained something called DNA. Suddenly, human beings could be understood in a whole new way. Likewise for Socrates, absent were the myriad of silly gods and their petulance toward one another and humankind. Suddenly present was a divine spark inside of every human being that relates essentially to the body it is present in, but then lives on, and moves on after the body dies. As Plato recounts again toward the end of *The Republic*:

> Socrates: "Aren't you aware that our souls are immortal and never perish?"
>
> Glaucon looked at him in astonishment. "No, really? I was not aware of that. Can you really prove such a thing?"

He does, and the immortal soul is born, the most powerful religious idea ever suggested, what many theologians over the last twenty-five hundred years have called "a point of such importance that it includes all the truths of religion."[5]

Not that it is universally accepted. No great idea ever is. In the sixteenth century, for example, the Protestant Reformers Martin Luther and John Calvin disagreed about the soul's immortality. Luther said that no one is conscious after death because everyone waits for the final bodily resurrection. In other words, a human being doesn't exist in any way, shape, or form without a soul (an idea he derived from Thomas Aquinas). Calvin countered that souls were immortal while bodies waited to resurrect. Similarly, even in ancient Greece, the immortality of the soul was not applauded by everyone. Epicurus, who came along a century after Socrates, said, "Death is no concern of ours, because when we are alive, death is not, and when death is our reality, we are not." But Dante would place Epicurus, and everyone like him who denies the immortality of the soul, in Hell's sixth circle.

One reason why this idea has persisted is surely that the notion of the soul's essential difference from the body seems to resonate with human experience. We are all born full of potential, and most of us grow steadily with bodies prepared for a long and healthy life. But before we breathe our last, those bodies have often broken down to the point where it feels as though the soul or spirit is most of what is left. In fact, the soul often feels more complete than it ever has in those moments before the body dies, as if a person is ready to move on without the body weighing it down any longer.

Plato's *Phaedo* is the beginning of many things in religious history, including a view of the afterlife that says each soul does not so much get what it deserves as it receives what it wants. It was C. S. Lewis who once said that most souls, were they to suddenly go to Heaven, would probably feel somewhat uncomfortable there. A good life is supposed to prepare us to be at home with goodness. In Plato's case, however, this idea verges on the wacky at times, as when Socrates offers it as an explanation for the existence of ghosts: "This...may explain why some souls are depressed and dragged down again into the visible world, because they are afraid of the invisible and of the world below— prowling about tombs and sepulchers....They continue to wander until the desire which haunts them is satisfied and they are imprisoned in another body." He then offers some thoughts about how such souls may transmigrate—a gluttonous one into the body of an ass, a violent one into the body of a wolf, and so on. Not all of Plato passes the test of time!

PLATO'S IMPACT ON PAUL

The apostle Paul would make good use of the immortality of the soul three centuries later while writing letters that became part of the Christian New Testament. He was a firm believer in the soul's immortality and its essential relationship to the body during a human life, but also in its ultimate separation from the body after death—ideas that differ markedly from what Paul would have learned in school when he studied the Torah.

Paul was a genius. He was also a devout Jew, well-schooled in all manners of ancient thought, and a respected first-century thinker in the eyes of Epicurean and Stoic philosophers, according to Acts 17. He knew his Plato, and Greek philosophy had an unmistakable impact on his writings. For example, Paul would agree with Plato in affirming each of these ideas to be the God's truth:

- The soul is a pure spiritual essence.
- It contains nothing material, nothing that is essentially of this world.
- It is uncreated and eternal.
- After death, the soul once again belongs to the world of the invisible.

In contrast, a Moses, a King David, or a Jeremiah wouldn't have had the slightest clue what those statements are supposed to mean!

If you know Paul's writings, you'll remember how he seems to often distinguish vividly between the body and the soul, such as when he says to the Corinthians reassuringly, "For though absent in body, I am present in spirit" (1 Cor. 5:3). Or later in Corinthians when he explains how he "punishes" and "enslaves" his body, so that it won't get in his way (see 1 Cor. 9:27). You only have to substitute "Christ" for "Philosophy" in these words of Socrates from Plato's *Phaedo* and you can almost hear the voice of Paul:

> Therefore they who care for their souls, and do not merely live according to the passions of the body, say farewell to all this. They will not walk in the ways of the blind. And when Philosophy offers them purification and release from evil, they feel that they ought not to resist his influence, and to him they incline, and wherever he leads they will follow.

And if you add the words "of Philosophy" after each instance of "Spirit" in this passage from Paul, you can almost hear Socrates: "Live by the Spirit, I say, and do not gratify the desires of the flesh. For what the flesh desires is opposed to the Spirit, and what the Spirit desires is opposed to the flesh" (Gal. 5:16–17).

The word for "spirit" (*pneuma* in Greek) in Paul means the innermost center of a person, the rough equivalent of Plato's "soul," but then Paul and Christianity add that this is where God the Holy Spirit takes hold of a person's life. (In contrast, the word usually translated as "soul" in the New Testament comes from the Greek *psyche*, which in turn comes from the Hebrew *nephesh*, meaning a "living being," not something immortal.) Both Plato and Paul agree that there is a clear way of salvation, and although their ways ultimately have different causes, the routes are remarkably similar. This led many medieval theologians to conclude how "all that was true in philosophy was but a presentiment and foreshadowing of Christianity."[6]

There are many occasions in the Epistles when Paul reveals his affinity for Plato, for instance: "This slight momentary affliction is preparing us for an eternal weight of glory beyond all measure, because we look not at what can be seen but at what cannot be seen; for what can be seen is temporary, but what cannot be seen is eternal" (2 Cor. 4:17–18). Also, "Of course, there is great gain in godliness combined with contentment; for we brought nothing into the world, so that we can take nothing out of it" (1 Tim. 6:6–7). And, "For now we see in a mirror, dimly, but then we will see face to face. Now I know only in part; then I will know fully, even as I have been fully known" (1 Cor. 13:12). We could go on.[7] Many of Paul's greatest hits were from the Greek philosophy back catalogue.

If you are an orthodox Christian believer, you probably never knew just how Greek you were. Even Paul's most famous one-liner, about welcoming the soul's release from the body at the time of death, wasn't an original. "I say that to die is gain," said Socrates in the *Apologia*, and then Paul: "For to me, living is Christ and dying is gain" (Phil. 1:21)! The idea of an ideal city, introduced by Plato in *The Republic*, also seems to be addressed in similar terms by Paul in his lengthy Letter to the Romans. Enough. The comparisons could go on forever. Simply put, Paul learned from Greek philosophy and made use of the immortality of the soul in the formation of Christian theology.

BEYOND PAUL TO DANTE

Early Christians then went on to incorporate soul immortality into their emerging theology. Clement of Alexandria and Origen are two of the most prominent cases before 250 CE. In 387 Augustine wrote an entire treatise titled "On the Immortality of the Soul." Medieval Christians were so influenced by Plato that throughout the era, cathedrals, scriptoriums, and monasteries are referred to as heavenly places that are similar to, but better than, the schools of ancient Athens. For centuries, Christian theologians pointed to Paul's words in Romans 1:21, saying that he was talking about some of the Greek philosophers when he said, "For though they knew God, they did not honor him as God." And so-called pagan authors like Pythagoras, Plato, Cicero, Horace, and Virgil were quoted and paraphrased, their words seemingly baptized as holy whenever necessary.

Dante, who knew Plato's writings translated by medieval Muslim scholars into Arabic, then rendered by Christians into Latin, would become the architect of all this by the later Middle Ages. He knew that without an immortal soul that is sensitive and fully conscious, separating from the body at death, Hell would make a lot less sense. The dead needed to be fully conscious of what was happening to them immediately after their bodies died. By the Renaissance, Erasmus would declare Socrates a saint, convinced that he both possessed the truth and knew it: the same truth that was "the Word," or Divine *Logos*, which Saint John says created the universe. A century later, the French Roman Catholic archbishop François Fénelon began an essay on the life of Plato by saying, "Plato, the sublimity of whose doctrine has procured him the appellation of *The Divine*…"[8]

I see evidence all the time, even in our own day, that

the Platonic notion of the immortality of the soul is still essential to Christian belief and practice. In fact, I think of it every time I go to Mass. Consider the language of the Catholic liturgy of the Mass as it was changed in 2012. Before approaching the consecrated bread and wine, the congregation used to say, "Lord, I am not worthy to receive you, but only say the word and I shall be healed." Now we say, "Lord, I am not worthy that you should enter under my roof, but only say the word and my soul shall be healed." It's as if someone wanted to remind us of the essential difference between body and soul.

FREE, FREE, SET THEM FREE

Ultimately, Plato's "soul" is untranslatable. "Inner life" gets closest, and if that's immortal, the possibilities of the afterlife are boundless. After Plato, the soul has become "the continuing existence of an inner, hidden part of the human person after death,"[9] and with this development came new understandings of what constitutes a human being both in life and in death.

Death itself was turned on its head. Poets and theologians began to imagine what happens as death approaches and the soul waits. An immortal soul, for instance, wouldn't be weary like a failing body would be. A soul might be anxiously awaiting a return to its source. To possess a soul became, then, almost like having a foreign element in one's body. Some have even imagined the glee a soul must experience as the body's death comes near. Others, simply the mystery of that moment of separation. One little known Renaissance poet, Francis Quarles, a contemporary of George Herbert, expresses this beautifully in a short verse:

My soul, sit thou a patient looker-on;
Judge not the play before the play is done:
Her plot hath many changes; every day
Speaks a new scene; the last act crowns the play.

According to the Hebrew Bible, a human soul couldn't be separated from its body. The Hebrew psalmist who cried out to the Divine was hoping to be saved in total—in a very real, immediate, physical salvation. When he says, "I lift up my eyes to the hills—from where will my help come? My help comes from the LORD" (Ps. 121:1–2), there's no deep spiritual meaning intended by the author of those verses. Come God, quick, I'm in trouble, is more like it! When a Hebrew psalmist wished out loud to God that God would ransom his soul from the power of Sheol, he knew that his body was still close at hand. Occasionally, one would sing to God that his life force, his spirit, would somehow be grabbed hold of and his spirit renewed—but that was a purely spiritual yearning. In either case, body and soul remained together. Not so in Athens four hundred years before Christ. A soul that separates from the body after death added to the complexity of what it meant to be human, and made the possibilities for afterlife endless.

CHAPTER SEVEN

Plato and the Myth of Er

FROM DANTE'S INDEX CARDS...

> Needed: Divine justice
> after death!

Eternal life alone isn't enough to explain the existence of Hell. After all, every human being after death could simply ascend to the Elysian Fields of Greek myth, a quiet place in the sky where plains of pleasure lie and verdant fields of Heaven may vie with ether and a purple sky. (I just narrowly misquoted from John Dryden's classic translation of Virgil's *Aeneid*.) It sounds a bit like dog Heaven, doesn't it? Well, in order to create an inferno for sinners, Dante needed divine justice, too.

Socrates challenged many assumptions of his society—some cultural, some ethical, pedagogical, political, and theological. He and Plato were part of what is called the Ionian Enlightenment—Greek poets, philosophers, and historians who altered the story of Homer and Hesiod. They included Xenophanes, who wrote that Hesiod and Homer didn't speak for everyone when their writings had the gods doing immoral, disgraceful things. These Enlightenment thinkers introduced ethics into the mythological view of the cosmos and the godly pantheon. People had to be ethical, and even gods had to follow ethical rules.

But bizarrely, and much to the disappointment of philosophical purists everywhere, Plato extends this talk of justice to the indeterminable, para-rational afterlife by retelling a strange tale at the end of his most famous book. References to an afterlife that's related to divine justice are fleeting in the New Testament, but the concept receives a full treatment at the end of Plato's *Republic*.

You may have read *The Republic* in college, but if you were a student like me, you probably didn't make it all the way to the end. It's in those last few pages—after goodness in this life is described as having its own reward here and now—that we see Plato conclude with the idea that a good person also receives certain rewards in the afterlife. This is where Plato's Heaven is introduced, offered up as the ultimate justice and end in the universe.

His primary intention was to explore what the perfect city might look like, in which people desire to do good and not evil, and where the just prosper while the unjust are rightfully punished. It has been said that for a society to function its citizens must be under legal obligation to follow certain laws, with the threat of penalties if they disobey, and that's the subject of *The Republic*. Plato believed there was a necessary connection between morality and democracy and that a community can never truly come together without a system of laws and punishments for those who break them.

But he wasn't satisfied to speak only of the laws and motivations that govern the ideal city here on Earth. Plato concludes with an odd myth, a supposed account, a secondhand tale, to illustrate the point that what governs a just society on Earth also governs what happens beyond the grave. In the final pages of *The Republic*, he introduces the idea of justice after death—and a divine judge (or judges) who will be there to sort out the righteous from the unrighteous. The odd "Myth of Er" not only depicts souls of the dead following the inclinations that they cultivated in life to the grave, but as being individually judged, and getting what they deserve in the eyes of God.

Prior to Plato, the dead were simply judged by the living. Friends, families, communities, and reputations were the collective judge of what sort of person someone was, for eternity. People's passions and sins were buried with their bodies, and their bodies and souls (the whole package) went to whichever after-hours place under the topsoil you choose. That's all that existed in the Hebrew Bible. Consider the threats and promises offered to the people of Israel: If they didn't follow the commandments of God, they wouldn't prosper, they wouldn't be blessed, and they faced severe retribution at the hands of the community (for example, a rebellious daughter could be stoned to death by her village). On the other hand, if they *did* follow the law, God would bless them and make their name great. God would curse anyone who cursed them, and bless their descendants so that they became a great nation—and that's only said to Abram in three verses at the beginning of Genesis 12. There's plenty more. All of this is what makes today's prosperity gospel preaching turn on a dime. What tremendous mileage they receive by encouraging people to claim these promises!

The Myth of Er wants to change this, because the soul appears to achieve victory over the body, purifying itself, or remaining pure in itself, so that when the body dies, the soul lives on, and being right before God is about more than simply what you've earned in this life.

EARLY GODS MADE TWEAKS

Plato had broached the topic of justice meaningfully on earlier occasions, most of all in a dialogue known as *Gorgias*. There the scene begins in the streets of Athens, with Socrates and his disciple Chaerephon meeting Callicles, who tells them of an exhibition they've just missed in which Gorgias was displaying his famous rhetorical skills. Socrates says that he'd actually like to talk with Gorgias about the art of rhetoric, and so they all walk over to Callicles' house, where Gorgias happens to be staying. There they talk, and the talk ranges from rhetoric to morality to political ambition and evil in the world.

Toward the conclusion of this wide-ranging conversation, Socrates is challenged by Callicles, who tells him that he seems to be living in another world with his idealism about personal morality. You see, Callicles is a realist and a materialist who believes that ambition, power, and persuasion, as long as they don't contradict the laws of the state, are what rule the world. Socrates responds by telling him, "To go to the world below, having a soul which is like a vessel full of injustice, is the last and worst of all evils." Then he continues to tell Callicles a story.

Socrates reminds him of how Homer in the *Iliad* speaks of the brothers Zeus, Poseidon, and Hades dividing up the cosmos among them, ruling the Heavens, the oceans, and the underworld, respectively. Then he says, "But in the days of Kronos," the father of those brother gods,

> there was this law respecting the destiny of persons, which has always existed, and still continues in Heaven, that he who has lived all his life in justice and holiness shall go, when he dies, to the islands of the blessed, and dwell there in perfect happiness out of the reach of evil, but that he who has lived unjustly and impiously shall go to the house of vengeance and punishment, which is called Tartarus.

Tartarus, you may remember, was the deepest place in Hell according to Greek mythology.

This is something new—the unjust being punished in the afterlife. Socrates goes on to say that judgment occurred, in days long ago, on the occasion of a person's death. And since both the people being judged and the unnamed judges themselves were alive, "the judgments were not well given." So Hades and "the authorities from the islands of the blessed"—like the representatives of two opposing political parties—went to Zeus to tell him that souls were finding "their way to the wrong places." Something had to be done to fix the system.

Zeus analyzed the situation, and his resulting diagnosis will probably make you laugh. The reason the judgments were inaccurate, Zeus explained, was because "the judged have their clothes on." Seriously. It's a metaphor. In other words, they were being judged in their earthly getups, as their put-on personae, and not, as one might say, naked as the day they were born. The old way had disregarded the age-old principle that justice is supposed to be blind. (Go to your local courthouse and see the statue of Lady Justice, a goddess from Egyptian and Hellenistic times, holding and balancing scales, with a blindfold covering her eyes.) Even better, Socrates goes on to say that he wants them judged as souls, not just bodies. "There are many having evil souls who are appareled in fair bodies, or wrapped round in wealth and rank, and when the day of judgment arrives many witnesses come forward and witness on their behalf, that they have lived righteously," he explains. In other words, the wrong things are being judged.

So Socrates tells his listeners that then and there, Zeus made changes. First of all, the living will no longer know when they are about to die. And those who die will be stripped of everything—clothes, rank, status, and friends— in order to face judgment. The judges, too, will be stripped; they will be without prejudices themselves. Here's how it will work: The dead will come together in a meadow. Their deeds and misdeeds will be considered, and rewards and punishments meted out. As a result, Hades may have been mostly a place where the dead play, but Tartarus grew to become a dreaded destination where punishments are assigned based upon crimes, and where a person's eternal torment is meant to show how much he resembles his misdeeds. None of this would be possible without the separation of body and soul. As the philosopher explains, "When a man is stripped of the body, all the natural or acquired affections of the soul are laid open to view."

The medieval vision of Dante was indebted to these ideas from the fourth century BCE. Even the notion of purgatory has its origins back in Plato and the *Gorgias*. "Now the proper office of punishment [after death] is twofold," Socrates explains to Callicles. "He who is rightly punished ought either to become better and profit by it, or he ought to be made an example to his fellows, that they may see what he suffers, and fear and become better."

REWARD AND PUNISHMENT

So before he ever writes *The Republic*, Plato has made it clear that justice matters for the afterlife and there will be a judge who scrutinizes our lives. Then he tells a story that purports to illustrate how this might work and look.

Plato relays the details of Er's life and experience as if they are absolutely true. He probably heard this tale secondhand, and it may have even been an old tale by Plato's time. This instance of steering into the realm of hearsay has actually caused some scholars to wonder what went wrong with the great philosopher. One condescendingly refers to the

Myth of Er as charming and poetic, and another comes out and calls it "one of the few really embarrassingly bad arguments in Plato."[1] As we read it today, it sounds like the stories we hear of people who claim to have had a glimpse of the afterlife, as they stood somehow, somewhere, between life and death, and then returned to the living to tell about it. That's what Er does. After mentioning "the prizes which are bestowed upon the just by gods and men in this present life," Plato says, "And yet...all these are as nothing in number or greatness in comparison with those other recompenses which await both the just and unjust after death."[2] To that end, he adds, "I will tell you a tale..."

Er was a soldier who was slain in battle and lay, together with others, dead on the battlefield for a total of ten days. After the combatants had gone and reinforcements had come to clean up the mess, the bodies were gathered up and taken away. Now, a dead human body will begin to stink after only one day, and will start to show visible signs of decomposition after about three. Some people noticed that Er's body hadn't yet undergone any decay. Still, he was placed on the funeral pile with the others.

While lying there, Er suddenly sits up. He begins to talk, to tell the story of what he saw after death. This is where Plato introduces what had been unheard of to the patriarchs, matriarchs, prophets, prophetesses, kings, and queens of ancient Israel: Er's soul left his body. While the body lay dead, the immortal soul traveled on a journey. "His soul departed...and...came to a mysterious place at which there were two chasms in the earth," Plato says. And there is where some of what Er saw is eerily similar to what we read later in the teachings of Jesus. Some of it also seems straight out of—you guessed it—Dante's *Inferno*.

APPROXIMATE DATES OF COMPOSITION

Plato's Republic:	375 BCE
The synoptic Gospels:	70 CE
Dante's Inferno:	1310 CE

On one side, Er sees two chasms leading down into the Earth. To his other side, he sees two chasms reaching into the Heavens above. These are offered as options, but then Er discovers that the choice is not his to make, or at least not now. For "in the intermediate space there were judges seated, who bade the just, after they had judged them, ascend by the heavenly way on the right hand, having the signs of the judgment bound on their foreheads; and in like manner the unjust were commanded by them to descend by the lower way on the left hand; these also had the symbols of their deeds fastened on their backs."

The judges tell Er that he's not yet destined for a life after death. Er is meant to live longer, to return to the living and tell them what he has witnessed with his own two eyes. He not only sees souls going into the Earth and up to Heaven, but souls coming back from both places. The ones that had been in the Earth are often weeping as they tell their friends what they had to endure, and the souls just back from Heaven are telling their friends of the blessed and beautiful things they saw. Every one was dealt the following justice: for every serious wrong done to another person, and for every great act of holiness, they received a judgment equal to ten times one hundred years (a possible human life span). So, most of the souls were traveling to and from one-thousand-year terms spent in either place. A few had been so awful in life that they would never return from Earth, and a few blesseds would never need to leave Heaven, while most spend a millennium in one or the other.

Then Er sees the souls line up and choose a new mortal life, ranging from animals to every conceivable sort of human being. According to its character, virtue, and a lot of luck (they cast lots), each chooses—and has chosen for it—a reincarnated life in order to return to Earth. So, you see, Plato creates a vision of judgment, sentencing, reward, and punishment, as well as rehabilitation and reincarnation that is occasionally mirrored in the New Testament, but ultimately ends up resembling the first two books of Dante's *Divine Comedy* (Hell, Purgatory) more than it does anything in the Bible.

PLATO'S "MYTH OF ER" AND JESUS' "PARABLE OF THE SHEEP AND THE GOATS" (MATTHEW 25)

Myth of Er

At death, every soul is judged.

Sheep and Goats

All will stand before the Son of Man.

Myth of Er

Those who did well stand on the Judge's right hand.

Sheep and Goats

The blessed (called "sheep") go to the right.

Myth of Er

Those who did poorly stand on the Judge's left.

Sheep and Goats

The cursed (called "goats") go to the left.

Myth of Er

The blessed go to Heaven.

Sheep and Goats

Those blessed inherit the kingdom of God.

Myth of Er

The unfortunate go into the Earth to Hades.

Sheep and Goats

Those cursed go into eternal fire.

Myth of Er

After a term in either place, each soul returns to Earth.

Sheep and Goats

N/A

Plato wants his readers to know that there is something beyond death. The Hebrew Bible (which was surely unknown to him) offered a picture of human beings possessed of body and soul, connected by life that comes from God; and when God took that life away the entire person went to Sheol to lead a shadelike existence. Plato sees something else. Plato separates the human person into two very distinctive halves, only one of which truly matters. Fever, disease, "or the knife put to the throat, or even the cutting up of the whole body into the minutest pieces, cannot destroy the soul," he explains. The soul cannot ever be destroyed by an evil person, one who does evil things. Everyone is immortal by virtue of having an immortal soul, even though in this life it has to be stuck inside a body.

Plato compares a soul at the end of a human life to a shell in the sea that has layer upon layer of incrustations marring its beauty and form. Death is a welcome liberation for such a creature because the true identity inside may escape. And God, or the gods, will reward one who pursues virtue in this life, who tries to avoid too much worldly incrustation, whose desire is to be like God, or godly. "The prize of victory which the gods give the just" is to allow its soul to follow its nature, Plato explains. By all of these means, Er—and by retelling his tale, Plato—claims to have discovered that there is justice after all for everyone immediately after death.

CHAPTER EIGHT

Jesus, Hades, and a Pit Just Outside Jerusalem

FROM DANTE'S INDEX CARDS...

> *Needed: A place where people burn like garbage*

On its website, the Israeli Ministry of Tourism refers to the Valley of Hinnom as "green and tranquil" with "beautiful views of the Holy Land—and some dark tales, too."[1] That's a surprisingly mild way to put it.

The Valley of Hinnom is a popular stop on many tours of the Holy Land. It was there, just on the southern edge of the Old City of Jerusalem, in the time of the ancient Israelites, that apostate Jews, Canaanites, and a variety of other awful people sacrificed their children to gods. Seriously. The Bible tells us so. Several groups paid homage to various local baals, and Moloch, the fire god of the ancient nation of Ammon (today's Jordan), in this despicable way. They seem to have believed that appeasing gods meant burning their daughters and sons in sacrificial fires.

These were not just crazy people. In some cases, they were seemingly ordinary citizens from ordinary walks of life that you'd think would know better. One of the earliest biblical references is to King Ahaz of Judah sacrificing his sons, as well as a grandson, in the Valley of Hinnom (See 2 Chron. 28:3; 33:6). Somewhat later, the prophet Jeremiah tells a similar story, sadly, over and over again. Here are the words of the Lord as proclaimed by Jeremiah to the people:

> I am going to bring such disaster upon this place that the ears of everyone who hears of it will tingle. Because the people have forsaken me, and have profaned this place by making offerings in it to other gods whom neither they nor their ancestors nor the kings of Judah have known; and because they have filled this place with the blood of the innocent, and gone on building the high places of Baal to burn their children in the fire as burnt offerings...therefore the days are surely coming, says the LORD....I will make this city a horror. (Jeremiah 19:3–6, 8)

In two other places, God adds through the voice of the prophet that not only is it an abomination to burn their children in the valley, but God never even imagined that such a thing was possible (see Jer. 7:31–32; 32:35). Jeremiah curses the child murderers, as well he should have, and he places a curse on Hinnom, too, while he's at it. The point is: This was an awful place with a horrendous legacy.

By the time of Jesus in the early first century, the Valley of Hinnom was well-established as a cursed place just outside Jerusalem with a constant fire burning. By then, people mostly disposed of their trash there, but Roman soldiers would also throw the bodies of criminals executed by crucifixion into the infamous pit. There was no other use for such a pitiful location with a sinister history that backed right up to the Old City, close to the Holy Temple.

Over time, in Hebrew, the name for Hinnom evolved from *Ge-hinnom* to simply *Gehenna*. GEHENNA is the word that Jesus uses. He refers to Sheol in the Gospels as a place for the dead, but he also does Sheol one better when he makes reference to the notorious Gehenna as a destiny to be feared. Beware, Jesus says, or you will end up there— right on the other side of town—in that place you know you don't want to know! "If your right eye causes you to sin, tear it out and throw it away; it is better for you to lose one of your members than for your whole body to be thrown into hell [Gehenna]," he preaches (Matt. 5:29).

The problem is, most Bible translations confusingly render the word Jesus uses as "Hell." It wasn't Hell, certainly not what we think of as Hell. It was Gehenna, a sick garbage dump that any resident of first-century Jerusalem would have known and avoided on dog walks or while strolling at night under a new moon. Any Jerusalemite could have pointed to Gehenna on a city map, and everyone knew that kids didn't play there after school. Jesus was speaking in metaphor. Just as he was when he added, "It is better for you to enter life crippled, than having your two hands to go into Gehenna, into the unquenchable fire" (Mark 9:43). The fire he referred to was no longer fueled by children being sacrificed to Moloch, but mostly by the garbage that was always burning there, just south of the Old City. We could trace the origins of Hell's fire to the ways people regarded this garbage dump in Jerusalem.

MYTHICAL AND REAL PLACES

Gehenna trips us up, as proper nouns often do. We saw earlier how the Greek proper noun *Hades* appears in the New Testament as "Hell," and that's also misleading. Another example is Tartarus. Tartarus was known to first-century Romans as the prison of the Titans and the deepest recess of Hades, nothing more. But the author of 2 Peter writes: "God did not spare the angels when they sinned, but cast them into hell and committed them to chains of deepest darkness to be kept until the judgment" (2:4).

That's not Hell, certainly not what we think of when we think of Hell. Whoever wrote this passage reached back to a mythological place in order to locate where it is that God tossed the rebellious and fallen angels before time began, for *Tartarus* is the word being mistranslated here. The text actually says, "but cast them into Tartarus."

In about 100 CE when 2 Peter was penned, there was not a sufficient concept of Hell to justify anything other than a mythological reference. Perhaps that is also the explanation for why Jesus uses mythological references, rather than teaching his listeners something new or real. Although he certainly made the afterlife more tantalizing with what he said, he didn't do much to expand on what first-century Jews already understood about its location and description. He certainly didn't with his references to Gehenna.

Jesus said things such as, "For the Son of Man is to come with his angels in the glory of his Father, and then he will repay everyone for what has been done" (Matt. 16:27), without offering specifics. He also said these famous words to Simon Peter: "You are Peter, and on this rock I will build my church, and the gates of Hades will not prevail against it" (Matt. 16:18), which have provided no end to the possible speculation, mostly about Peter's role in leading the early church. But Hades was simply a reference to what everyone knew from Greek mythology. The opportunities for filling in the missing details are enormous.

There is one more scene, however, that is the occasion from prime time used by Christians over the centuries to justify preaching and teaching about Hell from the Gospels. This is, in fact, the only time when Jesus does more than simply reference a place called Hades or Gehenna, and it comes when he tells the story of Lazarus and the rich man. The anecdote appears in only one Gospel (Luke 16:19–31), but you may know it from the scene in the rock opera *Godspell*, where the Gospel text is quoted almost verbatim.

"There was a rich man who was dressed in purple and fine linen and who feasted sumptuously every day," Jesus begins. We hate the rich man already.

"And at his gate lay a poor man named Lazarus, covered with sores, who longed to satisfy his hunger with what fell from the rich man's table; even the dogs would come and lick his sores." Sounds like the makings of a good philosophical parable.

Jesus continues: "The poor man died and was carried away by the angels to be with Abraham." In the Torah, a reference to being with Abraham after death would have been like saying that the poor man would "sleep with his fathers" in Sheol—but elsewhere in the Gospels we hear Jesus refer to seeing Abraham after death as a sign of chosenness (Luke 13:28–29). He adds, "The rich man also died and was buried."

Then, the next two words say it all. Quickly, the scene turns to that mythological place we've come to know well. Jesus says, "In Hades, where [the rich man] was being tormented, he looked up and saw Abraham far away with Lazarus by his side." This is the Hades where souls are tortured according to their sins by underworld guardians who relish the task. It is the place made famous by Homer, Hesiod, and Virgil.

Perhaps you know the rest. The rich man knows who Abraham is, and seeing Lazarus by his side, calls out to Abraham, begging for mercy, asking if Lazarus could bring him some cool water to quench his terrible thirst. Then comes a condition for judgment number one: Abraham tells the rich man that he received all good things during his life, and now Lazarus will receive the good in the afterlife. Plus, Abraham says, "Between you and us a great chasm has been fixed . . . and no one can cross from there to us."

The rich man begs once more. "Then, father, I beg you to send [Lazarus] to my father's house—for I have five brothers—that he may warn them." And then comes the condition for judgment number two. Abraham replies, "If they do not listen to Moses and the prophets, neither will they be convinced even if someone rises from the dead."

What do we have that's new in this story? Certainly not a picture of Hell that is any different from the mythological Hades. Even Christ's most fearsome words of judgment stop short of both Hell and Heaven: "Then he will say to those at his left hand, 'You that are accursed, depart from me into the eternal fire prepared for the devil and his angels.... And these will go away into eternal punishment, but the righteous into eternal life" (Matt. 25:41, 46).

If Hell were so essential to Christ's message, or intended to be the primary incentive for believing a certain way or doing certain things, wouldn't you think that Jesus would have laid it out more plainly? But he didn't, because perhaps, like Paul after him, Christ had no notions of a dreaded afterlife the likes of which Dante would create.

HELL'S COSMOLOGY

We live in a century when there seems to be no end to specific teachings about Heaven and Hell, their characteristics, wonders, and inhabitants; and this is all well beyond what the New Testament contained. The teachings of Jesus, Paul, and the early disciples and apostolic writers seem to be mostly limited to the notion that an afterlife exists. Not much else.

In fact, one might even argue that Hell appears to be

mostly an earthly domain and problem in the worldview of the Gospels. This might explain why there are nearly fifty instances in the New Testament of Jesus and the disciples exorcizing demons from people. Evil seems to have been very much alive aboveground, and much less so down below. At the very least, Jesus appears to be most interested in the evil in the world, rather than what will happen afterward.

By the third century, Christian theologians like Tertullian began to agree about the afterlife: It wouldn't begin until the end of the world itself. They preached that all of the dead (except martyrs, who flew straight to God in the sky) went down to Hades, deep in the Earth beneath our feet. Then, in the "last days," when Jesus would come again, all human beings would be judged. The righteous would be sent to Heaven while the unrighteous would stay right where they are. The cosmology is fascinating because it differs so little from what had come before. The ancient, pagan worldview in many ways became the Christian worldview of late antiquity and the Middle Ages—and this remained the common way of seeing things up until about the nineteenth century.

Greek mythology had planted the seat of the gods and goddesses in a comfy cloudy space just above Mount Olympus. At nearly 10,000 feet, Olympus is the highest mountain in Greece, located in the Olympus Range on the border between what is now Thessaly and Macedonia, not far from Thessaloniki, Greece's second-largest city. The view from the top is breathtaking, looking out on the Aegean Sea. But not many of the ancient Greeks climbed

Mount Olympus; they were frightened of it. They were mostly content to imagine it from below, and their imaginings took on special meanings. They would look up in the sky toward that great elevation, and just above it they would see gods.

Is it any wonder, then, that Dante conceived of Hell as a place on this planet? Where else could it possibly be, modeled as it was after Hades and Tartarus? Dante wrote of its wide-opening mouth, just below the surface of the Northern Hemisphere, and spiraling or funneling downward until it reaches the Earth's center or core. It is there that the ninth circle of Hell, and the greatest offenders of God, are to be found, surrounded by a lake of fire that closely resembles those awful fires of Gehenna, fueled once by children, and later by the bodies of innocent victims of Roman crucifixion.

CHAPTER NINE

Inventing Holy Saturday

FROM DANTE'S INDEX CARDS...

Needed: A confrontation between Christ and Satan in the underworld

Soon after the events of the Passion, the Resurrection, and the Ascension were finished, the first Christians must have paused and reconsidered the events of those days. They must have wondered: Where was Jesus in between the Crucifixion on Friday night and the Resurrection on Sunday morning? His body lay in the tomb—but, as God, he couldn't just cease to exist for thirty-six hours, could he? Where was his soul...his identity...his person...where was *he* while his body lay dead? If you think about it, Jesus was sort of stuck in Limbo on that day between his crucifixion and his resurrection; the body was dead, but the person was still very much alive.

The Gospel accounts—which can be very detailed about the last few hours of Jesus' life as he hung upon the cross—say not a word about what happened on the following day. Jesus died on Friday night. What happened all day Saturday? So the early theologians imagined what might have happened. This is where Christ destroys the gates of Hell, puts Satan in his proverbial place, and shows to the faithful that he's conquering death once and for all. Epic additions to an already epic weekend.

There is one brief speculation in one obscure book of the New Testament, 1 Peter, that at some point in time Jesus preached to spirits—to people who no longer had bodies. "[Christ] was put to death in the flesh, but made alive in the spirit, in which also he went and made a proclamation to the spirits in prison," the passage intriguingly states (1 Pet. 3:18–19). There have been thousands of explanations as to what that could possibly mean. There's no mention in the passage of the usual proper nouns of where spirits of dead people were believed to reside: Sheol or Tartarus or Hades. There is only that word *prison*, which we now know sounds more like Plato than anything else, referring to how the human spirit is imprisoned in the body rather than a place down below. For good reason, Martin Luther called this the most obscure passage in all the New Testament.

It has no precedent in the Hebrew Bible. We've seen psalms where the psalmist imagines calling out from Sheol, but never a biblical case of someone alive visiting the underworld. That's the stuff of Odysseus and Aeneas, not the Bible. The witch of Endor conjured up Samuel in order to speak to the living from the dead, but there is no story of the dead hearing from the living. Another psalm, one of the most beautiful songs of David, has him feeling so foolish, sinful, and shameful that he describes himself as deep in a mire, stuck in a pit, even in prison, pleading with God to save him, and by psalm's end we hear that God will indeed do that (Ps. 69). And in Psalm 70, it is David again who says, "Make haste, O God, to deliver me; make haste to help me, O Lord.... Make no tarrying" (vv. 1, 5 KJV). God has always been recognized by Jews, and then Christians, as one whose work is deliverance—that is, in fact, what the word *salvation* means.

So, what could have occurred on that day between the Crucifixion and the Resurrection when there was a dead body but never a dead God? Where was the soul of Christ for those hours? Many, long ago, decided that the prison mentioned in 1 Peter was Sheol, and that Jesus went there not to preach, but to lift the faithful—like King David—out. Tradition tells us that it was the original apostles themselves who composed the Apostles' Creed, and they included a line that has confused Christians for two millennia:

> **He descended into Hell.**
> On the third day he rose again from the dead,
> He ascended into Heaven, and sitteth at the right hand of the Father Almighty.
> From there he will come to judge the living and the dead.

Although there is no account of such a day and its events in the Bible, in the first few centuries of Christianity, theologians created what has come to be known as "Holy Saturday," the day when Christ freed many of the shades or bodiless dead that had been waiting for liberation for centuries. Holy Saturday was excluded from later creeds like the Nicene, but influenced Christians throughout the Middle Ages and is still retained, recited, and affirmed by millions every day, including Catholics (in both the *Catechism* and the Roman rite for the Mass), Anglicans, Lutherans, and Methodists.

THE APOCRYPHAL SOURCES

The Gospels not only are silent about Holy Saturday, but they tease us with strange allusions to bodies popping up out of the ground that may have been walking around that day after the Crucifixion. Film scenes of walking zombies and the dead suddenly coming to life might as well have been inspired by sentences such as these from Matthew's Gospel:

> Then Jesus cried again with a loud voice and breathed his last. At that moment the curtain of the temple was torn in two, from top to bottom. The earth shook, and the rocks were split. The tombs also were opened, and many bodies of the saints who had fallen asleep were raised. After his resurrection they came out of the tombs and entered the holy city and appeared to many. (27:50–53)

Except that we don't usually think of zombies as saint-like. Notice: There are walking dead strolling into Jerusalem, witnessed by many. Jesus' death wasn't just about Jesus dying. At the moment he died, death itself went crazy.

The Gospel of Luke also tells the story of Jesus' last moments before death, and it is in that Gospel where we read the conversation between Jesus and the man known to legend and Christian tradition as the "good thief." Jesus says to him, "Truly I tell you, today you will be with me in Paradise" (Luke 23:43). The chronology of that day we get from yet another Gospel, Mark, which says, "At three o'clock Jesus cried out with a loud voice, 'Eloi, Eloi, lema sabachthani?' which means, 'My God, my God, why have you forsaken me?' When some of the bystanders heard it, they said, 'Listen, he is calling for Elijah.' And someone ran, filled a sponge with sour wine, put it on a stick, and gave it to him to drink, saying, 'Wait, let us see whether Elijah will come to take him down.' Then Jesus gave a loud cry and breathed his last" (Mark 15:34–37). He "gave up the ghost," as the King James Version more memorably puts it. That was late on Friday afternoon. So Jesus and the good thief were in paradise that day.

We have to move beyond the Bible in order to find the true precedents for the events of Holy Saturday. Those biblical passages are obscure and inconclusive. One memorable precedent is from the classics once again, this time the Roman poet Ovid (43 BCE–17/18 CE), who was of the same generation as Joseph, Mary's husband and the father of Jesus. Ovid was the bawdy author of a massive poem of mythological tales, *Metamorphoses*, written in the same

111

metrical style as Homer and Virgil. Some of the characters that appear in Ovid's poem appear also in the *Iliad* and the *Aeneid*. One of Ovid's most poignant tales comes in book 10 of *Metamorphoses*: the story of Orpheus, singer of divine songs, descending to the underworld to try to reverse the fate of his wife, Eurydice. (It is poignant, at least, until the end when he looks back at Eurydice, against the orders of the gods, as they're about to cross the border into upper Earth and she's consequently pulled back down to the underworld for good, to die a second death. Then Orpheus sings of loving young boys and orgies with women. But I digress.)

Eurydice had stepped on an adder and suffered a bite that killed her. Orpheus, after mourning "sufficiently in the upper air...bravely went below," which Ovid calls "this unattractive kingdom," to entreat Proserpina and Pluto, Roman goddess and god of the underworld "and master of the shades."[1] Orpheus brings along his legendary lyre and sings so sweetly, the text reads, that even the Furies are brought to tears for the first time. And he almost rescues his wife. Almost.

Christ would do Odysseus and Orpheus one better. Much better. Christ would enter the underworld to not only rescue a few (although that's an essential part of the Holy Saturday story), but to tell Satan that he is there to destroy death itself. And given that he is about to do that, so the thinking goes, those undead zombie saints who are coming out of their tombs just after Jesus died on the cross are given more context: they know something that the frightened residents of Jerusalem do not. Saturday has come!

Holy Saturday is the primary subject of an apocryphal text from the third and fourth centuries called the *Gospel of Nicodemus*. This text, which is now almost completely unknown outside books of medieval lore, was once widely influential and seriously, piously believed by Christians for centuries as almost another Gospel. It lays the legend out of what happened on Saturday most dramatically. Its anonymous author attempts to "fill in the gaps" of what the Bible does not explain.

The scene is set by a council of devout Jewish leaders who are discussing the events of the last several days, marveling over reports they are hearing of strange things happening throughout Jerusalem and beyond. They receive a report that the two sons of the high priest Simeon, Karinus and Leucius, whom everyone knew had been dead and buried long before, were now said to have come back to life (among those mentioned in the Gospel strolling into Jerusalem), residing in nearby Arimathea, "crying out, but silent as dead men." In the *Gospel of Nicodemus* we meet them, risen from their tombs, as they speak for the first time, telling their tale to Annas and Caiaphas, Nicodemus, Gamaliel, and Joseph of Arimathea, after the Resurrection and the Ascension. The elders find Karinus and Leucius kneeling in prayer; they embrace and kiss them, and take them to Jerusalem to the synagogue. There, they prepare a proper scene for truthful testimony:

> They shut the doors and took the Law of the Lord
> and put it into their hands, and instructed them by
> the Lord God of Israel who spoke to our fathers

by the prophets, saying: "Do you believe that it is
Jesus who raised you from the dead? If so, tell us
how it happened."[2]

With that, after making the first sign of the cross in history (upon their tongues), the brothers reveal:

We were all together with our fathers down in
the deep, in the obscurity of darkness, when all
of a sudden there came a golden heat like that of
the sun, and a purple, royal light came shining
upon us. Immediately before us was the father of
the whole race of humankind, and with all the
patriarchs and prophets rejoicing, we were saying:
"This light is the author of everlasting light that
promised to send us his co-eternal light."

This is the powerful scene of Holy Saturday. No wonder
it has been taken up by so many artists over the years!

Next, the sons of Simeon say, their father appeared
before them, and he told them to glorify Jesus Christ, the
Son of God, reminding them that he (Simeon) had held
Christ in his hands in the Temple as an infant, and declared
him the Messiah and the glory to come for the people of
Israel. "And when everyone heard these things, all the
saints rejoiced even more," the sons tell their elders.

The drama continues, in great detail, with one character
after another appearing. Along comes John the Baptist, saying that he prepared the way of the Lord, announcing Jesus
to be the Son of God when he baptized him on Earth—and

that now he will announce his coming even down here, below! Then Adam appears, and essentially says to his son Seth, *This is what I told you would happen one day in the future!* You see, Seth had gone to the archangel Michael when his father, Adam, was dying to ask for healing oil from the Tree of Mercy. It was denied him, for the archangel told him then:

> Don't worry yourself with tears, praying and begging for the oil of the Tree of Mercy, so that you might anoint your father Adam with healing for the pains of his body. For you will not be able to receive it until the last days, only when five thousand and five hundred years have passed. Then, will the most beloved Son of God come upon the earth to raise up the body of Adam and the bodies of the dead.

They had to be raised up out of Sheol. Then the *Gospel of Nicodemus* says, "Seth and all the patriarchs and prophets heard these words and called out with a great rejoicing!" I'll bet they did! One imagines a lot of hooting and hollering that day.

So it was taught to the Christians of the early church long before Dante's day that Christ rampaged and plundered Hell of all the prophets and patriarchs who were predisposed to believe in him, even though they lived before Christ was in the flesh. The Son of God, in his resurrected power, went down into Sheol and pulled out all of those who were God's friends, sitting in the darkness, to quickly see the light once again.

THE LEGEND CONTINUES TO GROW

But Christ did more than that, too. Throughout the Middle Ages, Holy Saturday became the subject of many other legends and texts, including a popular form of medieval literature and theater known as mystery plays, which were also sometimes called miracle plays. These were works of drama and piety intended to inspire Christians to faithfulness. They first appeared in the tenth century and were written and acted often by clergy and vowed religious. Then in 1210 the pope passed an edict to forbid clergy to act onstage, leaving mystery plays to the work of a passionate laity. Their action was conceived on a cosmic scale, and apocryphal legends were incorporated into the biblical story so that a series of plays would tell the grand design of the universe from the "Fall of Lucifer" to the "Last Judgment." In such a sequence, "Holy Saturday" would be performed between the death and burial of Jesus and the Resurrection.

In one play, the image of Christ on that mysterious Saturday is so bright that it is the image of Christ at the Transfiguration itself (Mark 9:2–8). Thus, old Moses calls out, "His body was as white as snow, / And his face was like the sun to sight; / No one on earth was so mighty / As to look directly into that light."[3] To some, this seemed like a fulfillment of what was offered in Isaiah 9:1–2: "But there will be no gloom for those who were in anguish.... The people who walked in darkness have seen a great light; those who lived in a land of deep darkness—on them light has shined."

Christ pulls them from the cavern to go to Heaven with him, leaving others to stay put.

But then there's added drama in these plays. They often depict a Christ who is not simply descending to Sheol to pull some of his friends out of the Earth, but is facing the evil opposition with dramatic dialogue. Most mystery plays set this scene at the gates of Hell itself. Before reaching them, Jesus has to battle demons that stand in his way, sometimes literally throwing them aside. And once he reaches the iron bars, he yells to Satan, "Open up, you Prince of Pain!"[4]

Satan responds, "Who dares to be so bold as to speak to me in such a way!"

In one play, a demon answers Satan's question with these words, spoken as if hissed at the feet of his dark master: "It is the Jew that Judas sold, for to be dead, the other day." The drama is almost irresistible. Jesus is of course victorious.

Christ proclaims in one play, "This place stands no longer stuck! Open up and let my people pass!" and Satan opens the gates, knowing that death no longer has the power it once possessed, but resolved to keep at it nevertheless. In other plays, Jesus tramples the gates like an elephant walking over a Volkswagen. All of this explains how a eucharistic prayer from the ancient church could say— in one breathless sentence—that Christ accepted death in order to "abolish death and rend the bonds of the devil and tread down hell and enlighten the righteous and establish the limit and demonstrate the resurrection."[5]

In one more play, Jesus orders Satan, "Undo your gates, you prince of pride!" And then adds, "The king of bliss comes in this tide!" as he enters without them being opened. In every case, those who are left behind are now no longer in Sheol; they are behind Hell's gates, lorded over by an even more embittered Satan.

Dante imagined all of this in the *Inferno*, beginning in canto 3 as he and Virgil walk through the ominous gates of Hell. Then, as Virgil begins to guide him through Hell's first circle, they see famous patriarchs and matriarchs from the Hebrew Bible milling about. They acknowledge Adam (not Eve); Abel (not Cain); Noah (not his sons); Moses (not Miriam); and several others. The scene goes like this, with Dante-the-pilgrim asking and Virgil answering:

> "Tell me, my Master, tell me, thou my Lord,"
> Began I, with desire of being certain
> Of that Faith which o'ercometh every error,
>
> "Came any one by his own merit hence,
> Or by another's, who was blessed thereafter?"
> And he, who understood my covert speech,
>
> Replied: "I was a novice in this state,
> When I saw hither come a Mighty One,
> With sign of victory incoronate."
>
> (canto 4, 46–54)

And several more, then, are named who left this place on that special occasion long ago, not by their own merit, but "by another's."

Each, Virgil explains, would have had to remain there

if it wasn't for what Jesus Christ did after the Crucifixion, when he made his solitary way deep down into the Earth, into Sheol's cavern, to raise them up. The Longfellow translation sometimes employs an unhelpful syntax and old word choices, and "With sign of victory incoronate" is one such occasion. Much better is "crowned, with the sign of victory."[6] More than twenty biblical figures are named specifically by Virgil to Dante who were taken on that memorable day, including:

> *David, king,*
> *Israel with his father and his children,*
> *And Rachel, for whose sake he did so much,*
>
> *And others many, and he made them blessed;*
> *And thou must know, that earlier than these*
> *Never were any human spirits saved.*
>
> (canto 4, 58–63)

So, why were these taken and not others? Because, it is said, they believed without yet knowing in whom to believe. They had the imagination and the will of faith. Their dedication to God was such that it somehow mysteriously included Christ without naming him. Or, in some equally mysterious way, they knew Christ without knowing his name. The theologian Thomas Aquinas called it "implicit faith."

This event is also known to Christian tradition as the "Harrowing of Hell," for *harrowe* is an Old English noun meaning "an uproar." "Such harrow has never before been heard in Hell!" exclaims one demon to another in a medieval mystery play.[7] "Harrowing" was also a farming term meaning to break up and disturb the soil, and how apt an image that is for Christ's bursting open the earthen bars of Sheol. As Virgil explains to Dante, "[Christ] made them blessed, / And thou must know, that earlier than these / Never were any human spirits saved" (canto 4, 61–63). In other words, Sheol had never released a soul until that mysterious day between the Crucifixion and the Resurrection. And when the soul of Christ had done Saturday's good work, it rejoined the body that lay in the tomb, so that both body and soul might rise on the third day.

CHAPTER TEN

Medieval Apocalyptics!

FROM DANTE'S INDEX CARDS...

> *Needed: The world*
> *coming to an end*

It sounds like a new event in the Olympics, doesn't it? Apocalyptics. I think I just made the word up, but if there'd been an Olympic Games during the Middle Ages and if writers were ever invited to participate as athletes (*What a sentence!* the crowd roars), medieval apocalyptics would have been the event to garner the largest crowds. They were a serious pursuit, with rules like a game that captivated the imaginations of millions who believed that they had a life-or-death stake in the outcome.

"Apocalypse" comes from an ancient Greek word, *apocálypsis*, which literally means "uncovering," but also "unveiling" or "disclosure," as in secrets being revealed. And as you probably realize, the last book of the Bible sometimes goes by that name in addition to the "book of Revelation" or the "Revelation of Saint John," the latter being the name given for its author in the text itself. So apocalyptic literature began with the last book of the Bible and all of the bizarre images and references that are found in it. Just in case you've never read Revelation, here is a quick sampling of the visceral, dreamlike, and surreal that you'll find there:

- The Son of Man wearing a long robe and with a golden sash across his chest. His voice is "like the sound of many waters" (1:13, 15).
- A sharp, two-edged sword protruding from the mouth of the Son of Man (1:16).
- References to Satan's throne, as well as his synagogue, existing somewhere on Earth (2:13; 3:9).
- A slaughtered Lamb with seven horns and seven eyes (5:6).
- Someone riding on a white horse holding a bow; someone else on a bright red horse holding a sword; then a rider on a black horse holding a pair of scales; and a rider upon a pale green horse whose name was Death (6:2–8).
- The full moon turns to blood, every star in the sky falls to Earth, and the sky itself vanishes from sight (6:12–14).
- A giant pregnant woman whose clothing is the sun, has the moon under her feet, and is crying out in the agony of giving birth (12:1–2).

- A red seven-headed and ten-horned dragon that waits to devour the giant woman's child as soon as it's born (12:3–4).
- "Flashes of lightning, rumblings, peals of thunder, an earthquake, and heavy hail" (11:19).

That's to name only a few, and none can be good unless you enjoy the last one because it's like the Weather Channel. Let's just say that all of those images are supposed to be interpreted allegorically, if at all.

This strange way of communicating spiritual ideas was not created by early Christians, but earlier, by Jews. There are plenty of apocalyptic passages in the books of the Hebrew Bible, including Isaiah, Joel, and Jeremiah; and then there were dozens of apocryphal apocalyptic writings also written by Jews during the first two centuries CE. These have titles like "The Apocalypse of Adam," "The Apocalypse of Abraham," and so on, as many of them are what's called pseudepigraphic, meaning they weren't written by who they say they were written by.

Both Christians and Jews were intensely persecuted at times between 60 and 300 CE under emperors like the notorious Nero. These persecutions came in the form of the destruction of the Jewish Temple in Jerusalem, throwing Christians to the lions in the Roman amphitheater, and various other ways that people of both faiths were scapegoated, hunted, or murdered. This understandably gave rise to scary visions of what was to come because it was a comfort to dream of getting away from their present situations through some sort of divine victory. Revelation says in its opening line that the events being foretold "must soon take place," and then a few lines later, "Blessed is the one who reads aloud the words of the prophecy, and blessed are those who hear and who keep what is written in it; for the time is near" (1:1, 3). But from the relative comfort of wherever you are as you read these words right now, you'd be in a very select group if you felt blessedness after reading the secrets revealed in those pages. Most of us would rather they'd stayed under wraps.

Early Christians believed that Revelation was speaking to them and their generation, and the world was on its last legs. Similarly, no human effort can affect history, the apocalyptics proclaim, because the end of all things and the end of each of us will come by divine irruption.[1] As a result, every apocalyptic poem or treatise is littered with references to the afterlife and Hell, as the authors worried about, dreamed of, and imagined the end just around the corner. All of these strange texts show that Dante was not the first Christian to speak of Hell as a place for eternity at the end of time, not by any stretch of the imagination.

GOLDEN ERA FOR THE DEATH OF THE WORLD

In late antiquity, before Christianity was favored by the Roman Empire, the faith was outlawed and Christians were severely persecuted. During Diocletian's reign (284–305), for instance, thousands who professed faith in Christ were murdered by the Roman state in the most horrible ways. At these times, apocalyptic games reached a high pitch, as "the end" must have felt particularly or desirously near.

Early on, there was the Apocalypse or Revelation of Peter, written in Greek in the late second century, perhaps somewhere in Egypt. The setting is a common one in all the early apocalyptics: The scene begins with a group of early disciples of Christ listening to "secret" teachings from him after his resurrection. These secrets are told to one disciple in particular—in this case, Saint Peter. What is told centers on the afterlife and what it is like in Heaven and Hell.

In the Revelation of Peter, Jesus says that Heaven is full of people with milky white skin and bright clothing, and who celebrate their happiness together in joyful song—in other words, a stark contrast to the disease, filth, and bleakness known to most residents in the average second-century Mediterranean town. Hell, in contrast, is described by Christ as full of people being punished according to their sins.

We see the same sort of "tit for tat" and "eye for an eye" that characterized much of the Hellenistic and medieval worldview of how sins are rewarded in the afterlife, a worldview that Dante inherited and made full use of. For example, in the Revelation of Peter, blasphemers are in Hell hanging by their tongues, and adulteresses are hanging by their hair. Idolaters are seen by Peter hitting one another with rods of fire. Before their conversation and journey to Hell are over, Jesus tells Peter that all people will likely be saved from Hell by the love of God and the prayers of the righteous in the end. Then Peter turns to his son, who is named Clement in this apocryphal account, saying,

"Don't say a word about this, because if they know they may sin even more."[2]

There was also an anonymous and apocryphal Apocalypse of Paul, most likely written by a Syrian or Egyptian monk in the fourth century as an extension of the Revelation of Peter. It, too, discusses Hell after offering a tour of Heaven. Heaven is again white as snow and filled with pious, harmonious song. And Hell is offered as a place where people get what they deserve. The coldhearted, for instance, are submerged in a river of ice.

Next, the tale told in the Apocalypse of Peter follows a slightly different story line and one that almost seems straight out of a slightly twisted version of Frank Capra's *It's a Wonderful Life*. The angel Clarence was sent to help guide George Bailey away from the precipice just as an angel of the Lord guides Saint Peter through this text, showing him a just man on Earth at the time of death going up to Heaven for his good deeds, followed by an impious man at the point of death going unclaimed by holy angels and falling to Hell. Here is a sample, as Peter tells what happened to him:

> The angel said to me: "Look again down on the earth, and watch the soul of an impious man who vexed the Lord day and night, as it goes out of his body. That man would say, 'I know nothing else but this world. I eat and drink and enjoy what is here, for who has ever descended into Hell and come back again to declare to us that there is judgment there?'"

So again I looked carefully, and I saw all the scorn of that sinner, and all that he did. It was all hanging over him right then in his hour of need, when his very body and soul were threatened with judgment. I said, "It would have been better for him if he had never been born."[3]

Like the others, this text was also forbidden reading for Christians throughout the Middle Ages, beginning with Saint Augustine's condemnation of it in the early fifth century, but there were also some medieval church leaders who endorsed it—and it was widely read and discussed "underground." We know that Dante knew about it, because in canto 2 of the *Inferno* when he writes of "the Chosen Vessel travelled [to Hell]," he's surely referring to this pseudepigraphic text. A few lines later, Dante-the-pilgrim protests going any farther, worried for his safety, saying, "But why should I go there? Who sanctions it? / For I am not Aeneas, am not Paul" (lines 28, 31–32).

Speculations and Revelations Grow

For centuries Christians added these accounts to the storehouse of their faith. St. Brendan's Voyage was another one that popped up in the early Middle Ages. In it, the popular Irish saint and his cohorts travel from place to place in a large Irish coracle, or boat, made of wattle, somewhere presumably in the North Atlantic, searching for the original

Garden of Eden. They are prompted to take the journey after another saint tells Brendan all about his own experiences in paradise. They occasionally land on a variety of unknown and strange islands, including one that's uninhabited but where food has been left out, another where a boy seems to live in solitary confinement, another with only sheep, one with a gryphon, another on which mysterious birds sing praises to the Lord, one that turns out not to be an island at all but the back of a whale, and another that is home to the famous Saint Paul the Hermit. Toward story's end, at least one of the islands, complete with a volcano, seems to stand in for Hell in the Celtic imagination, while next door to it on another island, Brendan finds Judas Iscariot resting in peace. The one who betrayed Christ is apparently allowed to escape from Hell's grip on Sundays and saints' feast days.

All of these texts were once commonly read and wildly popular among Christians. And since there isn't much new under the sun, sometimes their appeal was driven by how raunchy they could be. This was surely why Questions of Bartholomew became such a hit. Supposed to be a recorded dialogue between Jesus and the disciples, spurred on by Bartholomew saying to the risen Christ, "Reveal to me the mysteries of the Heavens," it also implies in one place that the original fall of humanity occurred because Eve had sex with Satan in the Garden. The Harrowing of Hell also has a reprise in this fascinating document, which dates from about the same time as St. Brendan's Voyage, when Bartholomew asks Jesus:

Lord, when you went to be hanged upon the cross, I followed you from far off and I saw you hung there, as well as the angels coming down from Heaven and worshipping you. But when there came darkness, I looked and I saw that you had vanished from the cross, and I heard only a voice in the earth below, and suddenly great crying and gnashing of teeth. Tell me, Lord, where did you go from the cross?

Jesus responds by telling Bartholomew that he truly glimpsed a blessed mystery, and Bartholomew repeats that he heard voices below, and asks, What were they? Jesus offers this accounting of holy mysteries:

When I had descended five hundred steps, the angels and the powers cried out: "Take hold, remove the doors, for behold the King of glory cometh down!" And Hades said, "O, help me, for I hear the breath of God!"

It's easy to see why these texts were so widely read during the Middle Ages, if not by ordinary people, who were usually illiterate, but by monks, the wealthy, and intellectuals in cities. What we call fiction today was once holy speculation. Also, the average person had access to precious little Bible reading, preaching, or theological teaching, and throughout the early Middle Ages even many a priest couldn't read or write. These were prime times for the power of the imagination, and these stories were told and retold to those without access to them in book form.

Other details are offered in Questions of Bartholomew, such as Jesus' answer to the question, How many people on Earth die each day? "30,000." And how many of those are found to be righteous? "Barely fifty-three."

At another point, the disciples ask Christ if they can see "the deep abyss," and attendant angels respond by literally rolling up the Earth like a piecrust so they can all peek underneath. But no real descriptions of the underworld are forthcoming. It simply says that they fell on their faces, and Jesus responded by saying, "I told you that you wouldn't want to see it!" Then one of the disciples—Bartholomew, again—asks Jesus if he can see Satan himself. Jesus begins by replying, "You bold heart! You're asking for something that you are not even able to look upon." But Bartholomew claims he's ready. So again the angels respond and literally drag Satan in his chains from Hell in order to stand before the disciples, who promptly drop dead at the sight. Jesus revives them all and puts Satan to answer Bartholomew's questions, which center around the legend of the fall of Lucifer and the various rebel angels who accompanied him.

FEAR IS A POWERFUL THING

Medieval Christians had their fill of apocalyptic speculation about the afterlife, beginning with imminent doom and ending with a growing fear of Hell. These were the equivalent of medieval best sellers, and somehow they seemed to explain the world in ways that made sense to people. As a result, theologians in the Middle Ages were conscious of Hell, the end of the world, and a future of pain and misery; and writing about these subjects grew from century to century.

In Rome, Gregory the Great, probably the smartest pope in history, wrote about Hell's pains in his big book on Job in the early seventh century. In England, the Venerable Bede reported many visions of Hell in his *Ecclesiastical History of English People* (731 CE). Most notably, Bede tells of an Irish bishop named Fursey who was famous for his dreams. According to Bede, Fursey's soul parted from his body long enough to visit a dark valley with four deadly fires, each tended by demons. One fire was named falsehood, another cupidity, another discord, and the last, impiety. By these four sins the demons were attempting to drag good people to Hell. And in France, there was also Bernard of Clairvaux, famous preacher of the Second Crusade and a doctor of the church, who often mentioned the suffering of souls in Hell in his sermons, asking his vast audiences to be careful that they not fall for those temptations on Earth that lead one to eternal damnation.

Finally, in early thirteenth-century Essex, England, there was an illiterate peasant named Thurkill who told a story to scribes who then wrote it down in Latin. His became yet another popular tale. Thurkill describes how Saint Julian the Hospitaller took him on a guided tour of Hell. They journeyed "eastward to the middle of the world" to a great church and monastery cloister where all souls are judged upon death, some sent to Heaven, others to the refining pains of purgatory, and some straight to Hell, where particular sins result in particular punishments. The sitting judges are Saint Paul and a devil. Each grabs the souls when they tip the scales toward one side—good or evil. When simple Thurkill is returned to the Earth, his journey done, he then resolves to share what he saw only because he believes that it will save some who are still living to hear it.[4]

With all of these sources at his disposal, Dante was able to gather fuel for the fierce anger and drama of his *Inferno*. The Harrowing of Hell by Christ had given Dante the resentful evil power that he needed Satan to be—a Satan who was whipped and embarrassed by Christ in his own house. Now, that Satan must want to punish humanity even more than before, as a replacement for what he cannot do to the Divine. The apocalyptics also gave Dante something else that was valuable: the end of the world to come—for in that end is an eternal darkness for all humanity that doesn't ever come to see the blazing, salvific light.

CHAPTER ELEVEN

Dancing on a Pin

FROM DANTE'S INDEX CARDS...

Needed: Angels and
demons everywhere

How many angels can dance on the head of a pin? If you know only one thing about the Scholastic theologians of Dante's era, it is likely you know that those guys spent so much time debating minutiae that they could have argued for days on end on that one subject alone. How might we describe an angel's locomotive powers? What do angels know of divine and earthly matters? Do angels hate sin? Can an angel love in a way that humans might understand love? On a subject that most of us today would say is so indeterminate that it isn't really worthy of speculation, Scholastic theologians went to great lengths to dissect and describe. Dante loved this stuff.

Today, asking *How many angels can dance on the head of*

a pin? is really just a way of critiquing the speculations of those like Thomas Aquinas and their way of thinking and processing theological questions. It is our way of saying how silly the speculations used to be. What could it possibly matter? They must have had too much time on their hands.

The truth is, this sort of contemplation of the heavenly beings did not originate with Aquinas and friends, but they were building on the work of centuries of theologians before them. And these questions all seemed important because the Middle Ages was a time when the divine was believed to be fully integrated with the human. The immaterial and material worlds were closely intermingled, and medieval people had every inclination to accept that divine activity was going on all around them all the time, in miraculous ways. This is why their theologians were prone to ponder angels—as well as an angel's arch opposite, demons.

For example, a classification system was created over time that comprised three spheres or hierarchies of angels, each with three orders of different types. Medieval theologians dreamed this up out of their religious passion. Their mindset was: If we are to love God to the fullest, we should aim to learn as much as we possibly can about who God is, and where and how we might interact with God's messengers all around us. Surely angels are there for good reasons. And why stop at what the Bible says? God endowed human beings with brains that fill our large heads, so why not use them? That they did. Then they had help from an ancient text that was written before any of the New Testament.

THE BOOK OF JUBILEES

There is scant evidence in Scripture of anything approaching what the Scholastics proposed, although you'd be surprised how many different types or names of angels are actually used in the Bible. Only two of the archangels, Gabriel and Michael, are given proper names in the New Testament, but throughout the Bible you'll find multiple terms used for "angel." Beyond the biblical mentions, what inspired these more elaborate categorizations comes from the Jewish book of Jubilees, written two centuries before Christ, retelling the stories of Genesis and Exodus using new concepts not found in the Torah.

You may have never heard of Jubilees. It is one of those pseudobiblical books known as pseudepigrapha that we glimpsed in an earlier chapter. These are books that were long ago ascribed to the wrong author. Nevertheless, most have been taken seriously, and sometimes reverently, by believers for millennia. Jubilees is sometimes called the "Lesser Genesis," since it is so concerned with the themes of the first book of the Bible. Its content is filled with angels, and subsequently with demons, too. The author presupposes to retell the account of Creation through the Exodus as if in Moses' own words, and divine beings pop up everywhere.

It is from Jubilees that the early church created many of its basic understandings of angels and their classes, types, and functions. Christians came to understand seraphim, cherubim, and thrones to be the three types of angels closest to God's heavenly seat, caretakers of God's throne; while ordinary angels and archangels are what mingle with us here on Earth. Jubilees also taught that there are angels of God's presence, as well as angels of sanctifications, angels presiding over the created world, and individual guardian angels. In fact, when Jesus says to his disciples that every child has an angel in Heaven representing him or her to God the Father—he may have been pulling this idea from the book of Jubilees. This odd text also turns the minor biblical character of Enoch into a major figure, because of his interest in the angelic world. Jubilees says that Enoch was the first man to learn the art of writing, from the angels, and that he then wrote down, at their instruction, the secrets of astronomy as well as the complete chronology of the universe. We could all benefit from such help!

WITH THE GOOD COMES THE BAD

Together with all of this angelology is a fair amount of demonology as well. Jubilees refers to angels being created on the first day of Creation, but also a certain group that was intended to instruct humankind is soon seen mating with female humans—against the rules!—giving rise to a race of giants. This is meant to be an interpretation of Genesis 6:1–4, a passage from the Bible that's so unclear it has baffled experts for millennia. Genesis 6:4 speaks of a time "when the sons of God went in to the daughters of humans, who bore children to them," and Jubilees explains that these were angels having sex with women. What came of these unions? According to Jubilees, the women gave birth to mysterious offspring that were the first demonlike creatures on Earth, and thus began the era of evil that God eventually decided to eradicate with the Great Flood.

There is one possible corroboration of this theory that appears elsewhere in the Bible—in the book of Jude, where we see a late New Testament author referring to "the angels who did not keep their own position, but left their proper dwelling" as an example of those whom the Lord "has kept in eternal chains in deepest darkness for the judgment of the great Day" (Jude 6). This definitely refers to an after-life more intense than Sheol. The angels-turned-demons, being something more than corporeal, were not simply asleep or abandoned down in the Earth; for some reason they were in chains waiting for future judgment.

But all in all, the Hebrew Bible barely mentions demons—only on a couple of occasions, and almost always in passing, as if the writers did not really believe what they were writing. For example, demons are described as what might exist in the wilderness beyond all that is good and is known. When the prophet Isaiah tells of the coming destruction of Babylon, he starts by comparing that kingdom to something his readers will quickly grasp, saying that it will become like Sodom and Gomorrah. Then he adds that it will never again be inhabited. Even "Arabs will not pitch their tents there," nor will shepherds lead their flocks anywhere near it. Instead, "wild animals will lie down there, and its houses will be full of howling creatures; there ostriches will live, and there goat-demons will dance" (Isa. 13:19–22). What fantastical lines these are! Surely, neither the prophet nor his readers had ever seen an ostrich, let alone a goat-demon.

Later in Isaiah, Edom replaces Babylon as the kingdom

foretold to doom, and once again a bad place is prophesied to be laid waste in tangible ways ("the owl and the raven shall live in it"), but then much less so: "Wildcats shall meet with hyenas, goat-demons shall call to each other; there too Lilith shall repose, and find a place to rest" (34:11, 14). Lilith was the name of a female demon in later Jewish folklore, Adam's mythical first female partner who had been too mouthy to remain in Eden, before Eve.

So a demon, in the Hebrew Bible and other literature inherited by the first Christians, was mostly a metaphor for dangerous uncertainty. Dante would use these mythical, demonic characters in the *Inferno* to stymie and terrify Virgil and his pilgrim at every turn. I'm talking about Charon, Minos, Cerberus, the Furies, Minotaurs, Nimrod, and Satan himself. Then a demon also became a name for something slightly more concrete: a sort of non-god or protective spirit, the false presence behind an idol. There is only one occasion that makes reference to a demon this way: in the famous "Song of Moses" at the end of the Torah, when Moses remembers Israel's history and how they "sacrificed to demons, not God, to deities they had never known" (Deut. 32:17).

The New Testament is somewhat different. As we've discussed in an earlier chapter, there are at least fifty references in the Gospels to Jesus and the disciples casting out demons. The most memorable occasion is the scene of two demon-possessed men (called "demoniacs") who are said to have just emerged from tombs, challenging Christ. "What have you to do with us, Son of God?" they shout at him (Matt. 8:29). Then they beg Jesus that if he's going to cast them out, to send them into a nearby herd of pigs. What a great Jewish joke that was! So

Jesus did as they requested. On another occasion when he cast out a demon, the scribes who witnessed it accused Jesus of being Beelzebul, or Satan, for having such power (Mark 3:22). Jesus also refers to demons as disembodied spirits seeking rest—like shades. He says, "When the unclean spirit has gone out of a person, it wanders through waterless regions looking for a resting place, but it finds none" (Matt. 12:43).

Both testaments remain mostly silent about demonology—the sort of theorizing about the origins, purpose, and destination of demons, evil spirits, and Satan that became common over the twentieth century, particularly among Christian fundamentalists looking for the return of Christ in the final days (apocalyptics in our own time!). Even in the baffling book of Revelation—which no one should ever consider a "guide" to anything—there are a few quick references to what is often called the binding of Satan, such as the description of a battle that took place in Heaven between the archangel Michael and his angels and Satan and the bad angels. The story concludes by saying, "The Devil…Satan, the deceiver of the whole world—he was thrown down to the earth, and his angels were thrown down with him" (Rev. 12:9). There…suddenly appearing once again…is Sheol.

This tale comes up again several chapters later in Revelation, like a reprise:

> I saw an angel coming down from heaven, holding in his hand the key to the bottomless pit and a great chain. He seized the dragon, that ancient serpent, who is the Devil and Satan, and bound him for a thousand years, and threw him into the

pit, and locked and sealed it over him, so that he would deceive the nations so more. (20:1–3)

There's myth once again, in the form of a dragon. And there again is the Garden of Eden, in the mention of an ancient serpent. But there really is no Hell, certainly not Dante's Hell.

How Big Is Your Pin?

So how many angels *did* the Scholastic theologians say could dance on the head of a pin? The truth is, they didn't. Thomas Aquinas wrote that it is always a mistake to talk about angels as if they are corporeal; and whether they stand, kneel, or dance on a pin or needle or across a continent is entirely their prerogative. Still, he wrote at length about what philosophers like Plato and Aristotle did, or didn't, think about angels, and he set out to answer questions such as "Does an angel know himself?" and "Does one angel know another?" and "Do angels know the future?"[1]

The world that nurtured Dante was full of miraculous possibilities and vibrant spiritual imaginations. To the medieval mind, angels and demons both seemed obvious and necessary. Their presence seemed to explain some happenings, and the texts and traditions of both Judaism and Christianity supported this worldview. In all of their interactions with angels, figuratively, theologically, and through their five senses, the realities of both Heaven and Hell were made more present to people in everyday life.

CHAPTER TWELVE

Dante with a Qur'an by His Side?

FROM DANTE'S INDEX CARDS...

> Needed: A scarier Hell
> than we have

Is it possible? Well...yes. I doubt that Dante was up on his Arabic, but the Qur'an was actually translated into Latin in 1143 by a scholar named Robertus Ketenensis, a name that is usually Anglicized to Robert of Ketton. The translation was undertaken at the request of Peter the Venerable, the abbot of Cluny. You can still see this Qur'an edition in the Bibliothèque de l'Arsenal in Paris. Robert titled his translation *The Law of Mahomet the False Prophet*, so he was obviously not attempting to create an objective piece of work. In fact, he created a highly inflammatory and inaccurate translation, exaggerating all the parts about jihad and minimizing the portions that read closest to the teachings of Christ. He also added hundreds of notes, purporting to explain the text to his Latin readers, only they were full of expletives such as "liar" and "extremely stupid." There is even at least one unflatteringly drawn portrait of the Prophet, likely done by someone later than Robert that makes the Prophet appear to be part man, part sea monster.[1] Perhaps Dante read this book. Many well-educated men with access to fine libraries in cities like Florence and Rome unfortunately did.

But even an accurate and sympathetic translation of the Qur'an would show how, of all the scriptures in the world to appear before Dante's time, Islam's were the ones that most resembled the vision of Hell in the *Inferno*. The Holy Qur'an and early Islamic teachings were strangely preoccupied with not some vague underworld or indeterminate afterlife, but an angry, burning, furious Hell.

Islam is a religious reform movement that started in 609 CE when the prophet Muhammad began to receive revelations from God, called *Allah* in Arabic, through the archangel Gabriel. Muhammad was forty years old when the revelations began, and they ended with Muhammad's death twenty-three years later. The message of Islam in the Qur'an is, first and foremost, belief in the one and only God, who creates and sustains the universe, who is living, eternal, and omnipotent, and to whom every human being owes faithfulness. From the beginning, strong emphasis was put upon returning to pure monotheism, as it was believed that Christianity had compromised its position through the teaching of the Holy Trinity. But the second most important message of the Qur'an is about the afterlife:

its existence, its promise, and its threat to those who do not believe. Pick up any edition of the Qur'an and you will find a reference to the afterlife somewhere on every page.

Islam was a conscious outgrowth of both Abrahamic traditions, Christianity and Judaism; and the Qur'an is full of references to, and praise for, the characters that are most revered in the Hebrew and Christian Bibles. It in fact traces a sort of history of biblical characters and creates a prophetic path that begins with Adam, declared to be the first prophet of God, and then ends the era of divine prophecy with what is communicated to Muhammad. In the midst of all this, some fairly specific teachings about a place deep in the Earth called Jahannam are included.

Jahannam is an Arabic (the Qur'an was revealed entirely in Arabic) version of a Hebrew word—one that we've already encountered: *Gehenna*, that place that was once simply a valley on the southern outskirts of the Old City of Jerusalem but then grew, as we saw between the prophet Jeremiah and the teachings of Jesus, into a well-recognized cursed place. In the revelations of God to Muhammad Gehenna → Jahannam had become a full-fledged proper noun meaning "Hell." In other words, Hell as a tangible, physical, otherworldly place really had its birth in the teachings of Islam.

Jahannam did not remain on the southern edge of Jerusalem. It moved back to where Sheol had always been: deep in the belly of the Earth. Islam is quite specific, in fact, about where Hell is located geographically. Throw a stone into its mouth and that stone will travel for seventy years before hitting bottom, the tradition says. Another teaching declares that once you are in Jahannam, it is so vast that you can walk for forty years in any direction before reaching its outer walls. Perhaps taking a cue from ideas that originated with Plato, souls are usually sent to Jahannam for a period of one thousand years. But different from Plato, nearly every soul goes to Hell for at least a short amount of time.

Since the Qur'an is full of references to Jahannam, so are the hadith. *Hadith* in Islam is a tradition of spiritual knowledge and interpretation that is similar to Midrash in Judaism, and really has no parallel in Christianity—at least not yet. The word is usually translated as "tradition" in English, and hadiths are records of the deeds and sayings of Muhammad, often reflecting on a verse from the Qur'an, usually from one of Muhammad's earliest companions. They are the rough equivalent of the oral Torah in Judaism. Hotly debated during the Middle Ages as to which ones were genuine and worthy, the corpus of hadith now constitutes an extension of divinely revealed understanding for Muslims. One hadith has it that 999 out of 1,000 people will be in the fires of Jahannam, having somehow failed the test of life.

Also different from Plato, but not entirely from Christianity, is the sense in Islam that some who go to Jahannam actually enjoy it there. They are sent to Jahannam because they deserve to go, but also because they are predisposed to like it, as opposed to being disposed toward what is good, holy, and right. So some people remain in Hell for a longer time than others—simply because they cannot detach their desires from that which is no good for them. There's a bit of wise, what we might call "modern," psychology in that, and it wasn't foreign to Dante.

Jahannam actually is only one of the words for "Hell" in the Qur'an. There are others that translate into English as "Scorching Fire," "Abyss," and "Crushing Pressure." But in most English translations, all of these descriptive names are rendered as simply "Hell."

Sometimes the Qur'an deals with Hell in ways that sound similar to when the New Testament alludes to the second coming of Christ. The parallels are probably no accident: the revelations of Allah to Muhammad are full of borrowings from Christian Scriptures, just as Christianity borrowed from and reinterpreted Hebrew ones. To take one instance, sura 78 of the Qur'an describes the coming "day of decision," which is already known to God and will come at "an appointed time...when the trumpet shall be blown...and the Heavens shall be opened...and the mountains shall be moved."[2] Then it says, "Hell is an ambush, a reward for the outrageous, where they will be for ages."

We now know to see Sheol in the parallel passage in the New Testament, which appears in 1 Thessalonians 4:16–18, and to notice that there is no place of punishment, or what we've come to know as Hell from Dante, in these words of Saint Paul: "For the Lord himself, with a cry of command, with the archangel's call and with the sound of God's trumpet, will descend from heaven, and the dead in Christ will rise first. Then we who are alive, who are left, will be caught up in the clouds together with them to meet the Lord in the air; and so we will be with the Lord forever. Therefore encourage one another with these words."

The parallels between Hell in the Qur'an and what Dante uses to build his vast *Inferno* are stunning at times. There are seven levels, or gates, for sinners in Islam. There's a blazing fire designed to torment. And there's eternal loneliness for the worst sinners, comparable to falling into a great abyss. Horrible characters assist in the horrible work. Nineteen angels are charged with tormenting sinners in Jahannam, chief among them one called Maalik, just as every Dante reader encounters the myriad mythological creatures that punish sinners in the *Inferno*, from centaurs and the three-headed dog, Cerberus; to Minos, the son of Zeus who, according to Virgil in the *Aeneid*, judges souls in Hades.

COMPARING JAHANNAM WITH DANTE'S HELL

A place for those who committed sins against others, but also for unbelievers

QUR'AN: *Unbelievers are chief among sinners in the Qur'an. There are many verses that relate this. For instance, Allah relays, "Say to those who misbelieve, 'You shall be overcome and driven together to Hell.... God bears witness that there is no god but He.... But whoever disbelieves in God's signs, truly God is quick at reckoning up" (sura 3:10–19).*

DANTE: *Virgil explains to Dante as they walk through the first circle of Hell and see figures such as Plato and Galen, "They sinned not; and if they merit had, / 'Tis not enough, because they had not baptism, / Which is the portal of the Faith thou holdest; / And if they were before Christianity, / In the right manner they adored not God; / And among such as these am I myself" (canto 4, 34–39).*

Varying Levels of Punishment for Varying Levels of Sinners

QUR'AN: *Behind seven gates, designed for varied sins (sura 15:43—44).*

DANTE: *Sinners are contained in nine gradually lowering circles. This is a strange departure for Dante from Christian tradition about the afterlife. Christian teaching traditionally has no varying levels of any kind in Hell, but only, according to the bizarre vision portrayed in Revelation, "a bottomless pit, and from the shaft rose smoke like the smoke of a great furnace" (9:2).*

Fires That Are Fueled by Human Bodies

QUR'AN: *One of the most famous passages of the Qur'an is the one that says if you don't believe what Allah has revealed to the prophet Muhammad, call your witnesses who aren't God to make corrections. And if you can't, and of course you can't, "then fear the fire whose fuel is men and stones." The "stones" are a reference to idols (sura 2:23—24).*

DANTE: *There are many examples of this in the* Inferno*. For one, the sixth circle of Hell features heretics, Epicureans as well as various political and religious figures, trapped in flaming coffins (canto 10).*

Bodies That Are on Fire, but Not Consumed

QUR'AN: *Most memorably, Allah explains that for "those who disbelieve in our signs, we will broil them with fire, and whenever their skins are well done, we will change them for other skins, so that they may taste the torment some more" (sura 4:56).*

DANTE: *As they approach the City of Dis, surrounded by the river Styx, where the walls are made of iron and the people trapped within are burning, Dante-the-pilgrim remarks to Virgil from the valley above that he sees something vermilion-colored down there. Virgil responds tragicomically, "The fire eternal / That kindles them within makes them look red, / As thou beholdest in this nether Hell" (canto 8, 73—75).*

Lower Places in Hell for the Worst Offenders

QUR'AN: *In Islam, the worst offenders are hypocrites. The Qur'an says that as for hypocrites, there will be "none to help them" (sura 4:145).*

DANTE: *The lowest place in Dante's Hell is for the treacherous, the malicious, and traitors, such as Lucifer and Judas Iscariot (canto 34). Hypocrites are actually in the second-to-last circle in Dante, together with thieves and seducers.*

Hell isn't really about God's justice in Islam. It isn't even so much about God's vengeance. Instead, damnation (which is never "eternal," for only God can be that) is for the same purposes as the church made purgatory for during Dante's day: purification. All people must come to see God clearly, and to believe, before too long. So sura 75 has Allah saying, "I need not swear by the resurrection day! I need not swear by the self-accusing soul! Do people think that we shall not collect their bones?" And a powerful hadith says, "He shall make men come out of hell after they have been burned and reduced to cinders."[3]

VIOLENT RETRIBUTION MADE SENSE TO A MEDIEVAL FLORENTINE

Many Muslims today, particularly Sufi Muslims, de-emphasize or reinterpret these passages from the Qur'an and hadith about Hell. In this way, progressive Muslims are similar to progressive Christians. So the popular Sufi Lex Hixon was able to think of Jahannam as describing a dreamlike state, because the Qur'an elsewhere tells mostly of an all-compassionate and all-merciful God. "How could an all-compassionate Power create a realm expressly designed for beings to suffer even for an instant, much less for eternity?" Hixon questions rhetorically.[4]

But I imagine that the other, older Quranic worldview would have resonated deeply with Dante. Medieval Florence was a violent time and place, more so even than other parts of Italy. Religious Zealots were as common as political ones, and disputes in the piazzas over any subject often turned bloody. Earlier in the century of Dante's birth, the Inquisition was active in Florence, led by the charismatic Peter Martyr of Lombardy. He recruited groups of Florentine laypeople to maraud the streets seeking out heretics. We'd like to forget what was done to such unfortunate people at the hands of Christians who believed they were devout, but the sites of thirteen-century public massacres are marked near many churches in Florence to this day. Peter himself died after he was clubbed in the head with an ax a dozen years before Dante's birth.

There was also little justice in the courts, and those accused of crimes were often convicted based on unsubstantiated rumors, or simply to appease one faction or another. Those convicted of being traitors were sentenced most violently; hangings, quartering, and even being buried alive were not unheard of. Sons and daughters were often held guilty along with parents, and families began to band together—cousins, in-laws, siblings—to become more powerful and to defend themselves. Names like Cerchi and Donati, followed a century later by Medici and Tosinghi, were families to be feared.

The Middle Ages in Florence was a time when even political, military, and territorial battles took on theological significance. Islam was born in this milieu and so was Dante. In fact, Dante wrote an entire treatise, called *De Monarchia*, about the purpose of secular and religious power. Essentially he argued for "a return to the old dream of a worldwide Christian empire, governed in harmonious tandem by Emperor and Pope."[5] This is why he handed down many of his most bitter judgments to political ene-mies throughout the *Inferno*—they were thwarting the dream of a return to empire.

Jean-Paul Sartre famously said less than a century ago, "Hell is other people," and he might well have picked up the idea from reading Dante. You don't have to spend a lot of time learning about the political parties and ideological factions in Dante's Florence in order to pick up the salient facts that Dante's interpersonal relationships and profes-sional battles were significant, probably casting his perspec-tives on a wide range of issues. Many of his political rivals are easily found in Hell's circles. Read the notes at the end of each canto in any popular edition of the *Inferno* and you will see that many of the now obscure names are easily identified from the thirteenth century.

Dante fought, and fought hard; and when he lost, he almost died for it. That was the way of his world. Who the Guelphs and Ghibellines were, which Guelphs were "Black" and which were "White," who was aligned with the Holy Roman emperor and who with the pope, and when and why, will all make your head swim with details before long. The point is: Dante didn't begin writing the *Inferno* until he'd been exiled from Florence under threat for his very life. He was of a time when one's enemies were severely dealt with, and Dante was a political animal. So when his White Guelphs were outmaneuvered by the Black Guelphs, who were supported both religiously and financially by then Pope Boniface VIII, Dante was out. He was actually condemned to death on March 2, 1302—but he'd already fled. Dante got his revenge by placing Boniface in literary Hell for eternity.

As Elias Canetti once said, "In Dante's day, people were burned at the stake. When the other side came to power, you had to leave the city, and not come back as long as you lived. Hatred of the enemy *burned*."[6] So, too, did Dante's Hell. Whether he read the Qur'an in translation or not, he was a man of his time.

CHAPTER THIRTEEN

The Sublime Order of the Universe

FROM DANTE'S INDEX CARDS...

> Needed: If Hell exists,
> it must be logical.

Dante probably kept his pens in a pot on his desk. They were quill pens, made by first choosing strong wing feathers, then cutting back the flumes, and around the shaft ever so carefully with a penknife. Some quill pens take, hold, and flow the ink better than others, and I'll bet that Dante went through thousands of them during the years he spent writing the *Inferno*.

Preparing a new pen early one morning, I imagine him referring back to a sort of checklist of his intended source materials....

Note to Self: Use the following in creating my Hell.

- The lonely, abandoned sense of the Hebrews' Sheol underworld. Yeah, that'll be good.

- Use Virgil's pagan vision of afterlife. Maybe Virgil should even be my "guide," one great poet handing the mantle to another?

- Oh yes, and Homer's and Hesiod's god Hades. He's quite a character!

- Plato's Myth of Er, for sure, plus the Gorgias for what Socrates says about immortality of the soul.

- Definitely Christ slapping Satan around at the gates of Hell, and Satan growing ever more motivated to punish human beings because of it.

- Double-check the New Testament and teachings of Jesus, but don't think there is much there I can really use. Perhaps Revelation, though.

- Maybe a touch of Qur'an? They seem to have quite a retributive afterlife!

- Salacious rumors about my political enemies. Yeah, I'll be seeing them throughout the corridors of Hell!

- Aristotle's and Cicero's ideas of punishments might come in handy.

- And then of course I need some Thomas Aquinas and the Aristotelian order of the universe.

As we've seen, most of Dante's sources were the stuff of myth, legend, philosophy, and the politics of his day. In this final chapter, we briefly look at the "architecture" of his universe. By that I mean his view of how the world is organized and ordered, and how he carried that worldview all the way down to Hell. He turned mostly to the Greek philosopher Aristotle, the Roman philosopher and orator Cicero, and eventually to the "Doctor of the Church," Thomas Aquinas, for his answers. Let's work backward. . . .

DON'T KNOW MUCH ABOUT TELEOLOGY

If you happen to be Catholic, you probably grew up thinking that Thomas Aquinas (1225–1274) was like the fine silver flatwear that your mother removed from the mahogany cabinet on only the most important occasions. If you went to a liberal arts college, you probably have an image of Thomas Aquinas as chief of the medieval theologians. There was Augustine, and then there was Aquinas, the one who synthesized theology (faith) and philosophy (reason), taught popes, and became the "Angelic Doctor" during a time when philosophy and theology were one. The paintings you always used to see of him in encyclopedias and textbooks, and now on Wikipedia, show a Dominican friar who hasn't had to look very hard for his next banquet. But none of those images are what Dante would have known. In the opening decade of the fourteenth century when Dante was writing the *Inferno*, Aquinas was still a bit of a radical. He was the opinionated subversive of a generation earlier, teacher of university students, hero of freethinkers (hippies), and a professor who threatened orthodoxy by trying to mix it with so much pagan philosophy (mostly Aristotle).

Aquinas is called "Doctor of the Church" today, but he was called many, many much worse things during his years of teaching at the University of Paris. He was labeled a heretic on several occasions, and as a man who was sullying the pure gospel with corrupt ideas. Aquinas's ideas were hotly contested, and the real churchmen of his day thought the professor incendiary and dangerous to the minds of the youth. Some wanted to strip Aquinas of his priesthood and pulpit. Three years after his death, he was declared a heretic by one of his own: a prominent Dominican theologian in England who also happened to be the archbishop of Canterbury, Robert Kilwardby. Just a few days earlier, on the actual three-year anniversary of Aquinas's death, the bishop of Paris made his own list of heretical propositions—219 in all—that he said came from the mouths of the theology faculty in his city in recent years, most of them from Thomas.[1] He wasn't pronounced a saint until 1323, fifty years after his death, and two years after Dante's. And yet, "we do not know a Dante uninfluenced by Thomas Aquinas," writes Dorothy Sayers.[2] Aquinas's thought lurks behind the scenes throughout the *Divine Comedy*. This takes place mostly on a larger, overarching scale, by which I mean that Dante puts Aquinas's theological scheme to story—and both the scheme and the story are grand, cosmic, and universal.

Now, in order to approach Aquinas's work on nearly any biblical or theological topic, we could read dozens of volumes. His corpus was enormous. He was writing and dictating about three books at any given time, and it is said that his final output exceeded ten million words. So we can take only a breezy look at his thought, his philosophical

God are the angels, the higher orders of which move in the celestial spheres, the lower ones mingling with us. Then come the stars and the moon, followed by human beings, who are also made by God for the sole purpose of praising him. In this sense, although they reside upon the Earth, they are always, in their best moments, looking up, recognizing what Aquinas repeatedly calls "their ultimate end." After humanity come the creatures of the animal world, trees and plants, rocks and minerals. Each chain is connected to the one before it but also distinctly "lower" than the one before it, as designed by God. Everything ticks like a clock, relating constantly and intricately to the other parts of the universe like one grand mechanism.

Cosmologically, the Earth is the center of the universe, Hell is at the center of the Earth, and Heaven is above the clouds. This was often described like a great funnel cloud beginning above the stars where God resides, slowly making its way into terra firma and the field of human existence. It is not for us to ever know God in God's perfect form, high above us, but we come to know God in images and likenesses that are nevertheless real and meaningful. Everything around us is ordered sublimely and completely, kept ultimately in perfect symmetry by the magnetic attraction of the Divine high above, down through the images of God around us.

This cosmic orderliness includes the categories of humankind, as well. Kings and queens, for instance, are divinely instituted to rule over subjects; masters rule over servants; men rule over women; and the class, rank, gender, and wealth of every person is divinely planned, as each has a proper role to play in the grand production of life. When it is divine it is ordered, functioning smoothly; when evil sets in, we know it because the order breaks down. Imagine then, how it must have seemed when a child died young, or disease suddenly struck, or natural disasters occurred, or a man woke up one morning and simply decided that he wanted a different station in life. Every disorder was interpreted as the result of human fault or sin, as displeasing to God, a disruption of what the world was designed to be. Only disobedience or evil could result in mishap, confusion, misfortune, or disaster—or so they thought.

That perfect order included what is housed below the Earth's surface, as well, where God is never to be found. Satan was the supreme example of disorder and sin, hence the cacophony that evil creates in Dante's Hell. As this was explained recently by a professor at Georgetown who teaches the Scholastic view of the sublime order of the universe:

> "I shall not serve"... is the main disorder of the creature known as Satan. It also describes something about ourselves. Evidently, order in certain areas of reality but itself be freely chosen. But if order is rejected, as it can be, it is always rejected in the name of another order, even if it be one that has no origin except in ourselves. The great Augustine called it "pride" when we see no order in the universe except that which we construct for ourselves.[4]

Sin Ruins Us

Perhaps you are already able to detect how things go wrong for a human being in this worldview: We move away from God. Humans are placed in a tough spot according to the great chain of being. We alone, in all creation, possess both divine and animal characteristics. Like the angels, we are able to commit intellectual sin, such as pride, but animal-like we also can commit physical sins such as gluttony and lust. What the theologians explained was that sin shows us seeking "ultimate ends" that our souls might not otherwise select. Based on such principles, Aquinas created a vision of the afterlife in which Dante was well-versed. It is difficult to see it fully without reading the other two parts of the *Divine Comedy* (Purgatory and Paradise), but most of all, the poet learned that human beings are never exactly sent to Hell. Instead, it is by their actions, by the disposition of their will, that human beings who end up in Hell have essentially chosen it for themselves. It is that place and existence that they seek most of all—it's their teleology.

Still, there's also the sense—in both Aquinas and Dante—that God predestines some to salvation, and others not. Aquinas wrote in the *Summa Theologica* of "the plan in God's mind for how some people would come to salvation."[5] This is presented as a sort of sad reality that has no bearing on how a person lives his or her life; it simply explains that everyone's outcome fits the logic of the divine mind.

Once a soul does go to Hell, it has already earned a specific level of punishment, and its specific sins come to bear. For Thomas and Dante, the ordering of all things in the universe includes the eternal punishments that are meted out. As Aquinas wrote:

> The magnitude of each punishment matches the magnitude of each sin. For example, a sin that's against God is infinite, and the higher the person against whom a sin is committed, the graver the sin. It's more criminal to strike a head of state than a private citizen, and God is of infinite greatness. That's why infinite punishment is deserved for a sin committed against Him.[6]

Proportionality and order reign even here. The depth of a soul's deserts and desire are both determined by what it has done while embodied on Earth. And the greater the sin, the greater fondness the sinner will have for an eternity of misery. Perhaps he even, in some strange, sick sense, wants to be burned and beaten more than the others. This is more than a way of explaining divine justice. This is the anthropology of the sinner.

Dante believed with Aquinas that in every human being, the soul shares in what the body knows and experiences. A human is a composite being walking around the Earth, with a soul that descends from a pure form, with access to universal principles and truths that a body could never fathom, and a body that moves and emotes and uses its senses. Souls live on after the soul-body ceases, existing temporarily in a bodiless state while waiting for the ultimate resurrection when they'll conjoin with a perfected body. The spiritual anthropology of this is plain: One's body has a profound effect on one's soul, and that in turn can have eternal consequences, for good or bad. The two coexist in this life, working together. A soul can help you rise above your bodily appetites and focus heavenward, despite the worst of earthly circumstances or existence. But a body can also drag a soul down.

MORAL ORDER IN HELL

The idea of punishments matching sins originated long before Aquinas. Even before Christ, Heraclitus said, "A person's character is his fate," as if both were predetermined; and the Greeks and Romans had well-established understandings of which wrongs were worse than others and different grades of punishment for different crimes. They even developed hierarchies of what Christians would come to call "sins." So Dante's seemingly arbitrary assignments of punishments in the *Inferno* were nothing new—they followed ancient guidelines.

Still, Dante gave it a memorable name and rationale. In canto 28 he uses the Latin word *contrapasso*, which literally means "opposite—suffer," and is usually translated as "punishment." We've already seen this idea at work in the punishments that Dante-the-pilgrim witnesses being carried out throughout Hell when a soul's primary sin is closely related to the nature of the punishment it's receiving. The idea is as old as humanity itself: to each his due. This is why the first ring of Hell's seventh circle has those who were violent against others in life boiling in scalding blood for eternity. And in the second ring of circle seven, suicides are shown to become firmly rooted trees, a fate that is the antithesis to their desire in life to disappear. Harpies—bizarre bird-women from Greek myth—feed on their leaves forever, and it hurts.

For Aristotle, there were three basic categories in descending order of immorality: lack of self-control, sensual carnality, and then fully intentional and conscious malice. Upon this basic structure Dante places a host of moral faults and offenses, assigning punishments to each. Here is a sampling of them from the *Inferno*, in roughly the order they are presented throughout the descending circles of Hell. It is no accident that they seem arbitrarily assigned and malicious, making us want to better understand why certain sins seem to be so much "worse" than others. This is why we see...

Fault/Sin	Inferno *Punishment*
The unbaptized	forced to live in a blinding fog.
The lustful	who cannot extract themselves from a violent storm.
The gluttonous	with pestilent rain overhead, and worms underfoot.
The wrathful	fight with others in mud forever.
Heretics	bodies afire in their tombs.
Those violent against others	boiled in blood and shot by arrows.
Blasphemers	tortured with fire and scalding sand.

Fault/Sin	Inferno *Punishment*
The seducers	whipped by demons wherever they run.
Flatterers	buried in shit.
The corrupt	buried alive headfirst.
Thieves	attacked by snakes.
The fraudulent	surrounded by tongues of fire.
And traitors	heads down in the jaws of Satan forever.

Even if you think that Hell should exist, you might easily have disagreements with such a list. The fraudulent, for instance, are worse than the violent? That's not the case according to modern understandings of jurisprudence. And why would traitors be the worst of all human beings— condemned to be the farthest from God—as they are in Dante's lowest circle of Hell? The clearest answer to both questions may simply be, because Greek and Roman philosophers said so. Aristotle established most of these precedents, and also Cicero, the first-century BCE Roman philosopher. It was Cicero who wrote in *On Duty*: "While wrong may be done in either of two ways, that is, by force or by fraud, both are bestial: fraud seems to belong to the cunning fox, force to the lion; both are wholly unworthy of a human being, but fraud is the more contemptible." Then he added, "But of all the forms of injustice, none is more flagrant than that of the hypocrite who, at the very moment when he is most false, makes it his business to appear virtuous."[7]

LOVE ELUSIVE, LOVE DIVINE

By the time Dante-the-pilgrim makes it to the threshold of the Beatific Vision of God at the end of the last book of the *Divine Comedy*, it's become clear that knowledge will take a person only so far toward seeing God. All knowledge, Dante tells us, comes to an end and then love must take over. Love is what Heaven is about, it is what moves the planets in the sky, and only by love will we get there. This is also straight out of the medieval philosophers. It is love that actually moves the cosmos, according to the thought of the one that Thomas Aquinas refers to simply as "The Philosopher." Before Christ, Aristotle could see in the sky that the planets moved, and he imagined that their moving was out of a kind of love and affection for, and wanting to emulate and be closer to, the Unmoved Mover.

Diametrically opposed to the Beatific Vision, Hell is at the other end of the spectrum. So you see, there is a grand, cosmological design and logic to the entire universe, from God all the way down to the *Inferno*, and ultimately, love is used to explain it. Hell is what you might find in a place where there is no love whatsoever. Those who dwell there for eternity have essentially chosen their fate, because they knew no love in life. And yet, it is this perspective on love—in the cosmos, divine and human—that can also be deeply troubling in Dante's version. His understanding of love was—how shall we say?—screwed up. Here's why.

As I briefly mentioned at the beginning of this book, Dante experienced as divine the unrequited love of a Florentine girl named Beatrice Portinari. He tells us that he fell in love with her "upon first sight" when he was only nine years old and she was eight, in 1274. As he later remembers it in a poem called *Vita Nuova*, dedicated to Beatrice, "at that moment, I say verily the spirit of life which dwells in the secretest chamber of the heart did so quake that it appeared violently in my least pulses, and trembling said, 'Behold a god stronger than I who cometh to rule me.' From that hour forth, I say, that, Love ruled my soul."[8]

Don't pass too quickly over that important piece of information: Dante simply looked upon her as a child. The two most likely never even spoke to each other. Later, he tells us that she once passed him in the street when he was eighteen and "saluted" him, whatever that means. Dante describes all of this with the sort of fervor that resembles every first love. He was, for instance, "struck by lightning." As one Dante expert puts it, "She remained the love of his life, at least in his fantasies."[9] That's fine and good, and a lovely childhood memory, except that it became much more than that for him.

While Dante married another woman at eighteen and had several children with her, Beatrice also grew up and happily married another man. All the while she remained an obsession for Dante. One wonders what his wife and children must have thought. Then, when Beatrice died in 1290, obsession seems to have turned to an idealized passion. He romanticizes Beatrice, even almost deifying her, his unrequited love.

Some have suggested that Beatrice was not real at all, that she was a fictional creation meant to allegorically stand in for all of those things on Earth that draw us to God.

If so, Dante writes it incredibly realistically. By comparison, an allegorical meaning is intended by Francis of Assisi when he talks of falling in love with "Lady Poverty," but it is easier to understand Francis's love as allegory, seeing as there is no other human being involved, than it is to comprehend Dante's phantom experiences with a real flesh-and-blood woman.

At best, Beatrice is for Dante a symbol of pure goodness, purity, nobility, virtue, and love. At worst, she is a godlike figure. In the *Paradiso*, that third and final part of the *Divine Comedy*, even as the figure of Dante is about to look upon the Godhead, he finds that he can't take his eyes off Beatrice—the girl on whom he looked with love as a child. At this point I want to say, *Oh, please!* (But I also don't mind when Romeo and Juliet both finally expire at the end of their play.) What might have ended as an adolescent normality for most of us, in Dante becomes a grand bit of theological construction—essentially comparing the girl who won't have him to the God whom he also can never really touch, know, or love. Both Beatrice and God become mystical, impersonal sources of grounding love that "moves" the world (applying a little Aristotle to his psychosis) itself, even if that love won't give the poet the time of day. All of this makes for good theater, beautiful poetry, and a lousy way to understand how God relates to us.

Is There a Future for Hell?

There's a point in canto 9 when Dante interrupts the narrative stroll through Hell in order to tell his readers something important. It's like those moments in a Shakespearean play when the actor onstage turns toward the audience to address them directly. *Now, let me take a break from these proceedings in order to tell you something straight from the heart. . . .* Dante says:

> *O ye who have undistempered intellects,*
> *Observe the doctrine that conceals itself*
> *Beneath the veil of the mysterious verses!*
>
> (canto 9, 61–63)

By "undistempered" he means "sound." In other words, he's talking to smart people, and he's saying: Look closely here, because there is more going on than what's on the surface, "beneath the veil." This is Dante telling us to read his poem as allegory.

Merriam-Webster's defines an allegory as "a story in which the characters and events are symbols that stand for ideas about human life or for a political or historical situation." Pulling back the veil to uncover the allegories of Dante is what this book has been about from the start. And with that as your goal, you can study the *Inferno* for a college semester or a lifetime, exploring its allusions to classical literature, repurposing of Greek and Roman heroes, Christianizing of pagan concepts, and for the political and theological intrigue it recounts. Dorothy Sayers, the British mystery writer, rediscovered Dante that way during the London Blitz of World War II. "However foolish it may sound," she wrote, "the plain fact is that I bolted my meals, neglected my sleep, work, and correspondence, drove my friends crazy, and paid only distracted attention to [the bombs falling on London], until I had panted my way through the Three Realms of the dead from top to bottom and from bottom to top."[1] Dante's epic poem is powerful and beautiful and has had a similar effect on many a student over the centuries.

It can be a lot of fun when you read it on that level. That's why Sayers, again, could also refer to "the classical monsters [such as Minotaurs, centaurs, etc.] with which the *Inferno* is so pleasingly diversified."[2] Never mind the tasks and purposes that those monsters are given, were they to affect human beings that you or I might actually know; it is possible to enjoy simply discovering them. From Dante to Tolkien to Rowling, we love mythical creatures that do the most expected sorts of things, and reading Dante to find and identify them can be like literary detective work. All the allegorical passageways to meaning are fun to meander. You can almost take a course in ancient myth and medieval philosophy throughout its pages. But here's the problem: Millions of other people haven't treated what they've found in Dante's Hell as allegory. They've made it into gospel. When a Christian preacher threatens his audience with Hell, it is Dante's *Inferno* that he's most often depicting, whether he realizes it or not.

We must not forget that the *Inferno* is an allegory—rich with symbol and imagery that are to be understood on a variety of levels. Whether or not Dante considered his allegory to represent some sort of literal, historical, or geographical truth, let's just remember what it is, like when the Bible speaks of God's having a voice or living on a mountain. Surely the voice is a poetic reference to revelation, and the mountain means that God is majestic. In that case, is Dante's Hell still useful? Yes, great art brings things to life. Is it real? Yes, it can make sense in people's lives. But is it literal, historical, or geographical? No.

MY THREE COMPLAINTS

That's why my first complaint is not so much with Dante as it is with everyone who assumes that Hell, punishments for sinners, and Satan's wrath exist because of Dante. He tells us that his "mysterious verses" are allegorical, and yet many people take them as truth. The *Inferno* is more the stuff of Greek and Roman mythology and philosophy than it is the Bible, Old Testament or New. And all that myth and legend would be fine in and of itself (I love the classics!), except that Christians have adopted Dante's vision of divine justice and used it to threaten for centuries. *That* is the problem. Mythological characters decide the punishments and make up most of Hell's superstar inhabitants and torturers. So why have we read it as somehow spiritual? In contrast, if Dante had given us a taste of the afterlife only according to Scripture, we'd be left mostly with silence and mystery.

My second complaint with the *Inferno* is the virtues that it extols. Homer, Ovid, Cicero, and Virgil were more interested in heroism and courage than they ever were in peace and humility, and it is those latter virtues that Christianity and Christ are about. I'll take them, instead. I'll pursue those. This is why William Blake once exclaimed, "It is the Classics, & not Goths nor Monks, that Desolate Europe with Wars."[3]

And my third complaint with Dante is his politics. Church and state were one in his worldview. He couldn't conceive of them apart. He wanted to reestablish a new "Holy" Roman Empire, which in Dante's day was proudly discussed without the quote marks. Politics interested him, as did affairs of state and the repair of Rome as ruler of the world—more than the message of the Gospels. This is why it was common, just two centuries ago, to view Dante's poem as more of an "infernal freak show" of horrors than a genuine vision of the afterlife. No sensitive, spirit-inspired imagination could be so centered on wrath, noise, violence, and the sadness of ancient myth at its worst.[4] Dante was a poet who loved caesars and emperors, a man who would even have made a willing fascist, like the poets who extolled Dante's verse again in the twentieth century and called for its fulfillment under Mussolini.

HELL AND RELIGIOUS VIOLENCE

Hell has inspired many people to do good, or to do better with their lives than they otherwise would. That is the common argument for keeping Hell around. Dante's allegory reminds us that we are responsible, rational agents who choose every day between good and evil. That's why the *Divine Comedy* has been called "the drama of the soul's choice...deriving its power from the terror and splendour of the Christian revelation."[5] So should we keep Hell for this reason?

I became a Catholic at the age of forty-two for a number of reasons, and one of them was the official teaching of the church that a person does not know what will happen to him after death. "Faith combined with good works" is the old mantra of what it means to be a Catholic, as opposed to the view of the Protestant reformers of the sixteenth century who argued that salvation was about faith alone. The principle of "faith combined with good works" means that there is rarely ever a triumphant tendency among Catholics to proclaim any certainty about life after death. In fact, most Catholics believe that death and whatever comes after death are both part of a purifying process that's required before we ever meet God. Above all else, a Catholic has hope, and I believe that is the way it is supposed to be.

We need more than Hell as a deterrent, for ethics is not the same thing as loving your neighbor. Virtue is not borne out of fear. There have been awful people in history who have lived so-called ethical lives by following the rules. Also, for every person who has lived an ethical life because of the threat of Hell, there are ten whose lives have been ruined because the same threat was used as a way of wielding power over others—a power that is no person's to wield. Those who have held Hell's pitchfork over others' heads have created more Hell throughout history than they've helped others to avoid.

We read the *Inferno* differently today than people did just a century ago, before the horrors of wars, conflicts, and disasters were easily captured and documented by journalists and, most of all, photographers. Since trench warfare in World War I, can we still read of sinners dying slowly in fiery pits as God's divine punishment, as opposed to our own horrible mistake? Since Auschwitz, can we read of tearing and sizzling human skin and believe that it could ever be just? Can anyone read those portions of cantos 21 and 22 today where devils chase and gleefully torture shades without thinking of SS officers or Hutus chasing Tutsis? In Dante's era, the disturbing images in these and other cantos must have reminded readers of the most frightening examples of evil in their own era. Did they enjoy the poem for that reason? I don't.

In a scholarly paper first delivered in 1947, Dorothy Sayers said that Dante wrote in order to create visual pictures, "things that no mortal eye has ever seen," such as "the 'baked' skin of the sinners running under the fiery rain on the burning sand of Hell."[6] She must have not yet seen the photographs from Hiroshima and Nagasaki. The Second World War was transformative for anyone who desires to contemplate the afterlife. No one who experienced death camps or H-bombs firsthand would dare say that Hell is something worse to come, or that something as intangible as Heaven is the solution to such hellish horrors.

WHICH GOD DO YOU CHOOSE?

I haven't had much to say about God in this book because God is almost beside the point of Dante's *Inferno*. Hell is mostly about God's absence. But one of the things I've learned as I've grown older is that there is no single image or description of God that is the unvarnished truth. There isn't even one single image of God in the Bible, and each religious tradition contains a variety of images for the Divine. I've also come to accept that Christianity holds what seem to be contradictory images of God almost simultaneously. That's why I'm convinced that each of us has to choose.

There is, for instance, the God that Jesus preaches about in the Sermon on the Mount, who blesses the humble, rewards the meek, and promises the Earth to those who make peace instead of war. This is the Good Shepherd who will expend every effort to save a lost sheep from danger. This is the God that Saint Paul writes about when he beautifully says, "I am convinced that neither death, nor life, nor angels, nor rulers, nor things present, nor things to come, nor powers, nor height, nor depth, nor anything else in all creation, will be able to separate us from the love of God in Christ Jesus our Lord" (Rom. 8:38–39).

But then there is also the God of Jesus' parable of the Great Banquet (in Matthew 22 and Luke 14), in which the kingdom of Heaven is compared to a rich king putting on a wedding feast for his son. When none of the invited guests show up, he tells his servants to invite others to come; when they don't come either, he tells them to go out to the road and tell every passing stranger that they are invited to a feast. But when one man among these last invited guests shows up wearing the wrong clothing, the king is furious. Jesus says, "Then the king said to the attendants, 'Bind him hand and foot, and throw him into the outer darkness, where there will be weeping and gnashing of teeth.' For many are called, but few are chosen" (Matt. 22:13–14). This is the God who is compared to a king who rules his subjects, and who regards people as being like sheep and goats. This is the God we also encounter in Revelation, who seems to be looking forward to war and apocalypse, punishment and the ultimate outpouring of his own fury.

The *Inferno* offers only one of these images of God, and it isn't the one that I choose. All we have is a vivid, sad vision of a God who judges, punishes, tortures, and abandons. That doesn't make sense to me, and although those who have used Dante to preach Hell over the centuries have been able to point to a few biblical passages to support their ideas, they'd still be better stewards of the material to pull out a lexicon of Greek mythology. Ultimately, I choose not Dante's vengeful, predatory God who is anxious to tally faults, to reward and to punish. Instead I choose the God who creates and sustains us, who is incarnate and wants to be with and among us, and the God who inspires and comforts us. That God is the real one, the one I have come to know and understand, and that God has nothing to do with medieval Hell.

FINAL THOUGHTS

Dante would be pleased if we still feared his vision of Hell, as earlier generations of Christians certainly did. Much of the *Inferno*'s power in centuries past was derived from its threatening hand. In Dante's native Florence, for instance, the fire-and-brimstone Dominican preacher Savonarola held crowds of ten thousand captive in the Duomo in the fifteenth century with Dantean descriptions of Hell. So did Jonathan Edwards in his famous "Sinners in the Hands of an Angry God" sermon in early eighteenth-century America. But perspectives have changed. I don't think that's why we still enjoy the *Inferno* today—not because we find the descriptions or the threat of Hell to be compelling, motivating, or true.

If Dante Alighieri is "the chief imagination of Christendom," according to a line in a poem by W. B. Yeats, then that explains why it is tough to connect with so much in his *Inferno* today. His vision is an artifact of the past because we live today in a world beyond Christendom, something he couldn't have imagined.

"Great poets mean what they say," wrote J. Middleton

Murry, and he's right.[7] The fiction of the *Inferno* is entirely intentional. As one of the most prominent Dante scholars explains, Dante "was a passionate Christian from the late thirteenth century who had a burden for truth-telling, an evangelical zeal. As a medieval layman, however, he had no pulpit to speak from." Poetry became his pulpit. He was also a bitter man, as we've seen, burned by politics, who had more enemies than friends, and a soaring poetic talent that allowed him to get back at them with a work that would live on forever—the ultimate payback. Thus, "from the shambles of his life he felt called to speak the word of the Lord like a prophet or apostle, to write something like a Third Testament for his own time and place and that would, like Scripture, 'convince, rebuke, and encourage.'"[8] None of that appeals to me, today.

Our divine architecture, both in this life and in the next, is taking on new forms. The cosmic God who dwells in the skies and gently, gravitationally points us toward heavenly things is gone. The God who dictates laws and mandates beliefs to human beings, saying that they'd better follow them or repeat them or else face judgment, is going away or gone. I believe that Dante is still important, but for a different reason: from the opening lines of his allegory, he depicts how a pilgrim—any and every one of us—cannot help but face the ultimate questions of life:

> *Midway upon the journey of our life*
> *I found myself within a forest dark,*
> *For the straightforward pathway had been lost.*
>
> (canto 1, 1–3)

I think we are drawn to the pilgrim and his epic journey because examining life's big questions and challenges is essential if we want our lives to be meaningful for ourselves and for others. And we're still drawn to what is most radical about Dante's project: the revelation of the pernicious effects of sin upon human beings, and the ways that Dante exposes hypocrisy in organized religion. After all, he even sentenced a living pope to Hell!

The twentieth-century Catholic monk and writer Thomas Merton summarizes, in language I can relate to, how images of Hell can still make sense: "If you want to understand the social and political history of modern man, study hell," he writes. Because "the reason why [souls in hell] want to be free of one another is not so much that they hate what they see in others, as that they know others hate what they see in them: and all recognize in one another what they detest in themselves, selfishness and impotence, agony, terror, and despair."[9] That's my allegorical spin on what hell is: life-threatening, collaborative, and impermanent.

This is why when I read the *Inferno* today, I read it as a story of this world and not the next. Then the allusions, descriptions, and characterizations ring truer than ever, as they cause me to see the world for what it is—or what it sometimes is—as well as my place in the big story. Perhaps I can even see, at times, how to descend into hell in order to find a future and better paradise. My image of God simply leaves little room for medieval Hell, even though life can become hellish the further away we are from doing God's work.

Maybe someday a new vision of the afterlife will emerge. I imagine it might be a vision that doesn't threaten and also doesn't make promises, that dreams rather than dreads what is to come, and that recognizes how inaccessible and mysterious life—not just death—remains to us. I even suspect that if I were to explore an emerging twenty-first-century understanding of life after death over those cappuccinos with Saint Paul near the Roman Forum, we'd be tracking together more than either of us would with Dante.

Acknowledgments

Many thanks to Wendy Grisham of Jericho Books for her encouragement and fine editing. Many thanks also to Dr. Mark Bosco, SJ, director of the Hank Center for the Catholic Intellectual Heritage at Loyola University in Chicago. I was writing *Inventing Hell* during a busy time in life, and Mark graciously offered a summer office at the Hank Center, which I put to good use in 2013 as the book took shape. Lunches with Professor Michael Murphy, associate director of the Hank Center, who exemplifies the Catholic imagination in his own exuberant ways (including an affection we share for Morrissey and the Smiths, which I've now revealed to the world), were an added benefit.

Notes

Copyright Page

1. This is her own description. Mary Jo Bang, trans., *Inferno*, by Dante Alighieri, drawings by Henrik Drescher (Minneapolis: Graywolf Press, 2012), 11.

Prologue

1. Augustine, *The City of God*, in two volumes, trans. John Healey, ed. R. V. G. Tasker, introduction by Sir Ernest Barker (New York: Dutton, 1972), vol. 2, book 18, chapter 14. I have modified the translation slightly for readability.

2. This is the line from Dante that opens Bret Easton Ellis's *American Psycho*, unattributed.

3. Jorge Luis Borges, *Borges at Eighty: Conversations*, ed. Willis Barnstone (New York: New Directions, 2013), 10.

4. Mary Jo Bang, trans., *Inferno*; canto 32, 1–2, p. 305. For the second reference, see canto 12, 60–62, p. 113, as well as the note on p. 116.

5. He did the same when he created his other two mythical worlds of purgatory and paradise. Interestingly, it has been easy for Christians to understand Dante's purgatory as myth in recent centuries, but not his paradise. That's something for another book.

A Quick Sprint Through the Inferno

1. This insight/comparison originates with Robert Hollander in his note to canto 3, lines 1–9, from *The Inferno*, trans. Robert Hollander and Jean Hollander (New York: Anchor Books, 2002), 56.

2. Dorothy L. Sayers, *The Divine Comedy I: Hell*, trans. Dorothy L. Sayers (Baltimore: Penguin, 1950), 107. This comes in a note to canto 6.

Chapter 1: In the Beginning

1. Neil Forsyth, *The Old Enemy: Satan and the Combat Myth* (Princeton, NJ: Princeton University Press, 1987), 422–23.

2. For this perspective, which reveals an early Judaism that believes in much more than Sheol when it comes to the afterlife, see Jacob Neusner's chapter, "Judaism," in *Death and the Afterlife*, ed. Jacob Neusner (Cleveland, OH: Pilgrim Press, 2000).

Chapter 2: The Ancient Underworld

1. The first textual evidence of necromancy in ancient civilization occurs in Homer's *Odyssey* when Odysseus talks with the dead in the underworld. Interestingly, this sort of communicating with the dead, forbidden in the Bible, is what Dante's pilgrim does throughout the *Inferno*.

2. See Deuteronomy 32:22; 2 Samuel 22:6; Job 11:8; 17:16; Hosea 13:14; and Jonah 2:2.

3. See Job 24:19; Proverbs 1:12; Isaiah 14:11, 38:18; and Ezekiel 32:27.

4. See the fascinating thirteenth chapter of Umberto Eco's new book, *The Book of Legendary Lands*, trans. Alastair McEwen (New York: Rizzoli, 2013), 345–407.

5. John Berger, "Christ of the Peasants," from *Selected Essays*, ed. Geoff Dyer (New York: Vintage International, 2003), 533.

Chapter 3: The Awful Underworld Psalm

1. Christine Quigley, *The Corpse: A History* (Jefferson, NC: McFarland, 2005), chapter 6.

2. For the Pharisees, as for many Christians both early and now, where an afterlife is mentioned, "the whole person was to be saved, including the body. Therefore, such believers eschewed any notion of a salvation without the body. The language of 'immortality of the soul' is inaccurate insofar as it never appears in the NT." Jaime Clark-Soles, *Death and the Afterlife in the New Testament* (New York: T&T Clark, 2006), 39. As we'll discuss in a later chapter, the apostle Paul said many things that seem to contradict this.

Chapter 4: The God Hades

1. Alberto Manuel, *Homer's The Iliad and The Odyssey: A Biography* (New York: Atlantic Monthly Press, 2007), 1.

2. Homer, *The Odyssey*, book 11, trans. Samuel Butler, readily available online and in the public domain, for example: http://classics.mit.edu/Homer/odyssey.11.xi.html.

3. Short quotations from the *Theogony* are from Daryl Hine's verse translation in *Works of Hesiod and the Homeric Hymns* (Chicago: University of Chicago Press, 2007).

4. This is a definition offered by Bruno Latour in *Rejoicing: Or the Torments of Religious Speech*, trans. Julie Rose (Malden, MA: Polity, 2013), 3.

5. Peter Barnes, *Plays: 2* (London: Methuen Drama, 1996), 221.

Chapter 5: Virgil and the Myth of Empire

1. 4.3.

2. T. S. Eliot, *On Poetry and Poets* (New York: Farrar, Straus and Giroux, 2009), 143.

3. The line "Grief and the pangs of Conscience make their beds" comes from Robert Fagles's fine translation, *The Aeneid*, introduction by Bernard Knox (New York: Penguin, 2008), book 6, line 313.

4. *The Aeneid*, trans. Robert Fagles; book 6, line 352. You may have heard of, or even seen, the ancient tradition of placing a coin in the mouth of a dead person before they are buried. The coin was thought to be payment for Charon, the ferryman.

5. Robert Hughes, *Rome: A Cultural, Visual, and Personal History* (New York: Vintage Books, 2011), 17.

6. Virgil, *The Aeneid*, trans. Robert Fitzgerald (New York: Vintage Books, 1990), book 6, lines 1061–62.

7. E. H. Gombrich, *A Little History of the World*, trans. Caroline Mustill (New Haven, CT: Yale University Press, 2008), 74–75.

8. *The Dialogues of Plato in Four Volumes*, trans. Benjamin Jowett (New York: Scribner's, 1905), section 522. There are additional quotations from this dialogue of Plato later in the chapter; they, too, are from this source and can be found in sections 523–24. The only changes I've made are to replace the words *blest* and *wrapt* with *blessed* and *wrapped*.

Chapter 6: When the Soul Went Immortal

1. Homer, *The Odyssey*, book 1, trans. Samuel Butler, http://classics.mit.edu/Homer/odyssey.11.xi.html.

2. This is the Platonic idea of "absolutes," or pure "ideas" that literally somehow reside in the heavenly realm, independent and superior to the world of material things, and can be understood by only an unencumbered soul.

3. As before, I am quoting from the Benjamin Jowett translation of Plato, but I have made slight word changes here and there for clarity and sense.

4. Thomas Aquinas, *Summa Theologica*, part I, questions 54–58. Various editions.

5. Charles S. Stanford, trans., *Phaedo, or The Immortality of the Soul*, by Plato (New York: William Gowans, 1854), xxxix.

6. Etienne Gilson, *The Spirit of Mediaeval Philosophy: The Gifford Lectures of 1931–2*, trans. A. H. C. Downes (London: Sheed & Ward, 1950), 28.

7. See for instance, the book I cowrote with Phyllis Tickle, *The Age of the Spirit: How the Ghost of An Ancient Controversy Is Shaping the Church* (Baker, 2014). Even the doctrine of the Trinity is inspired more by Greek philosophy than it is by the Bible; on that specific point, see this interesting blog post by Tony Jones: http://www.patheos.com/blogs/tonyjones/2013/07/25/what-heresy-is-a-post-for-rachel-held-evans/.

8. Archbishop Francois Fenelon, "Life of Plato," in *Phaedo, or The Immortality of the Soul*, by Plato, trans. Charles S. Stanford (New York: William Gowans, 1854), ix.

9. James D. G. Dunn, *The Theology of Paul the Apostle* (Grand Rapids, MI: Eerdmans, 2006), 76.

Chapter 7: Plato and the Myth of Er

1. The first reference is to Simon Blackburn in *Plato's Republic: A Biography* (New York: Atlantic Monthly Press, 2006), 158. The direct quotation comes from this same page in Blackburn, op cit, but is quoting another scholar, Julia Annas.

2. All of the quotes from Plato in this early part of the chapter are taken from *The Republic*, sections 610–21 (at the tail end of *The Republic*), using Jowett's translation, with slight changes.

Chapter 8: Jesus, Hades, and a Pit Just Outside Jerusalem

1. At http://www.goisrael.com/Tourism_Eng/, visit the page for Valley of Hinnom.

Chapter 9: Inventing Holy Saturday

1. Ovid, *Metamorphoses*, trans. Charles Martin, introduction by Bernard Knox (New York: Norton, 2004), 341.

2. This quote, and others to follow, from the *Gospel of Nicodemus* are taken from an online English translation of the Latin available at earlychristianwritings.com, modified slightly for contemporary readability by the author.

3. From "The Harrowing of Hell," in *English Mystery Plays*, ed. Peter Happe (New York: Penguin, 1975), lines 89–92, p. 555. All of the translations of these plays began with this source, but are ultimately my own.

4. Ibid.

5. Quoted in *The Treatise on the Apostolic Tradition of St. Hippolytus of Rome*, ed. Gregory Dix and Henry Chadwick (New York: Routledge, 1992), 7–8.

6. *Inferno*, a verse translation by Robert Hollander and Jean Hollander (New York: Anchor Books, 2002), canto 4, 54.

7. Ibid., line 98, p. 556.

Chapter 10: Medieval Apocalyptics!

1. Bernard McGinn, introduction to *The Apocalypse in the Middle Ages*, ed. Richard K. Emmerson and Bernard McGinn (Ithaca, NY: Cornell University Press, 1993), 7.

2. Unless otherwise noted, translations from this apocalyptic text and others in this chapter are my own reworkings of those originally published by the great antiquarian and scholar M. R. James in *The Apocryphal New Testament* (Oxford: Clarendon, 1924).

3. Ibid.

4. See a sample in *Medieval Popular Religion 1000–1500: A Reader, Second Edition*, ed. John Shinners (Toronto: University of Toronto Press, 2009), 231–40.

Chapter 11: Dancing on a Pin

1. These are three of the questions in two of the chapters in the "On Angelic Knowledge" section of *Summa Theologica*. *Thomas Aquinas: Selected Writings*, ed. and trans. Ralph McInerny (New York: Penguin, 1998), 382–94.

Chapter 12: Dante with a Qu'ran by His Side?

1. Thomas E. Burman, *Reading the Qur'an in Latin Christendom, 1140–1560* (Philadelphia: University of Pennsylvania Press, 2007), 60–61. There was also published, in about 1273, a *Treatise on the State of the Saracens*, by William of Tripoli, a Dominican friar who lived in Acre. William's book offered a summary of the contents of the Qur'an, plus a brief overview of what was believed by Christians about the life of the prophet Muhammad. Among other things, William's book explained the popular medieval theory that Muhammad was a direct descendant of the wild and unpredictable Ishmael, referring to the characterization in Genesis 16:19. See *The Book of John Mandeville with Related Texts*, ed. and trans. Iain MacLeod Higgins (Indianapolis: Hackett, 2011), 235–46.

2. These quotes, and all quotes from the Qur'an, are taken from the great turn of the twentieth-century translation of E. H. Palmer, now in the public domain, and tweaked ever so slightly here to suit twenty-first-century taste.

3. This hadith is quoted in Cyril Glasse, *The Concise Encyclopedia of Islam* (San Francisco: Harper & Row, 1989), 153.

4. Lex Hixon, *The Heart of the Qur'an: An Introduction to Islamic Spirituality*, 2nd ed. (Wheaton, IL: Quest Books, 2003), 14.

5. John Julius Norwich, *The Middle Sea: A History of the Mediterranean* (New York: Vintage Books, 2007), 196.

6. Elias Canetti, *Party in the Blitz: The English Years*, trans. Michael Hofmann (New York: New Directions, 2010), 105.

Chapter 13: The Sublime Order of the Universe

1. Denys Turner, *Thomas Aquinas: A Portrait* (New Haven, CT: Yale University Press, 2013), 48–49.

2. Dorothy Sayers, *Further Papers on Dante* (New York: Harper & Brothers, 1957), 40.

3. Ralph McInerny, introduction to *Thomas Aquinas: Selected Writings* (New York: Penguin, 1998), xv.

4. James V. Schall, *The Order of Things* (San Francisco: Ignatius Press, 2007), 11.

5. Thomas Aquinas, *Summa Theologica*, 1a.23.2. I have slightly modified the translations of Saint Thomas for better readability.

6. Ibid., 1a2ae.87.4.

7. *De Officiis*, by Marcus Tullius Cicero, trans. Walter Miller, Loeb edition (Cambridge, MA: Harvard University Press, 1913), 1, 13, 41. I have changed a few words for clarity.

8. This is a translation done by Ralph Waldo Emerson in 1843. See *Ralph Waldo Emerson: Collected Poems and Translations* (New York: Library of America, 1994), 502.

9. Raymond Angelo Belliotti, *Dante's Deadly Sins: Moral Philosophy in Hell* (New York: Cambridge University Press, 2014), 4.

Conclusion: Is There a Future for Hell?

1. Dorothy L. Sayers, "...And Telling You a Story," in *Essays Presented to Charles Williams*, ed. C. S. Lewis (Grand Rapids, MI: Eerdmans, 1966), 2.

2. Sayers, *Further Papers on Dante*, 44.

3. In Milton Klonsky's *Blake's Dante: The Complete Illustrations to the Divine Comedy* (New York: Harmony Books, 1980), 14.

4. Ibid., 18.

5. Dorothy Sayers, *The Comedy of Dante Alighieri the Florentine: Cantica 1, Hell*, trans. Dorothy Sayers (Baltimore: Penguin, 1949), 11.

6. Dorothy L. Sayers, *Introductory Papers on Dante* (New York: Harper & Brothers, 1954), 1.

7. Quoted at the very beginning of Sayers's posthumously published book of essays, *Introductory Papers on Dante*, xiii.

8. Peter S. Hawkins, *Undiscovered Country: Imagining the World to Come* (New York: Seabury, 2009), 3.

9. Thomas Merton, from *New Seeds of Contemplation*, in *A Thomas Merton Reader*, ed. Thomas P. McDonnell (New York: Image Books, 1989), 65.

Bibliography

Dante Translations and Commentaries
There are hundreds of them. I have listed only those that I consulted more than twice. Others are mentioned in the Notes section.

Bang, Mary Jo (translator), *Inferno*, by Dante Alighieri. Illustrations by Henrik Drescher. Minneapolis: Graywolf Press, 2012.

Hollander, Robert and Jean (translators), *The Inferno*, by Dante Alighieri. Introduction and notes by Robert Hollander. New York: Anchor Books, 2002.

Longfellow, Henry Wadsworth (translator), *Divine Comedy: Hell*. This is the default translation used throughout this book and is widely available in the public domain, for example, at http://dante.ilt.columbia.edu/comedy/.

Palma, Michael (translator), *Inferno*, by Dante Alighieri, edited by Giuseppe Mazzotta. New York: Norton, 2008.

Raffa, Guy P. *The Complete Danteworlds: A Reader's Guide to the Divine Comedy*. Chicago: University of Chicago Press, 2009.

Sayers, Dorothy L. (translator), *The Comedy of Dante Alighieri the Florentine: Cantica 1 Hell*. Baltimore: Penguin, 1949.

Translations of Ancient and Medieval Sources (alphabetical by author)
Again, there are hundreds available for each author. These were my primaries.

[Apocalyptics] *The Apocryphal New Testament*, edited and translated by M. R. James. Oxford: Clarendon, 1924.

[Aquinas, Thomas] *Thomas Aquinas: Selected Writings*, edited and translated by Ralph McInerny. New York: Penguin, 1998.

[Augustine of Hippo] *The City of God*, in two volumes, translated by John Healey, edited by R. V. G. Tasker, introduction by Sir Ernest Barker. New York: Dutton, 1972. And *Confessions*, translated by R. S. Pine-Coffin. Baltimore: Penguin, 1961.

[Hesiod] *Works of Hesiod and the Homeric Hymns*, translated by Daryl Hine. Chicago: University of Chicago Press, 2007.

[Mystery Plays] *English Mystery Plays: A Selection*, edited with introduction and notes by Peter Happe. New York: Penguin, 1975.

[Ovid] *Metamorphoses*, translated by Charles Martin, introduction by Bernard Knox. New York: Norton, 2004. And, *Metamorphoses*, translated by Stanley Lombardo, introduction by W. R. Johnson. Indianapolis: Hackett, 2010.

[Plato and Socrates] *The Dialogues of Plato in Four Volumes*, translated by Benjamin Jowett. New York: Scribner's, 1905.

[Plutarch] *Plutarch's Lives, Volume 1*, the Dryden translation, edited with preface by Arthur Hugh Clough. New York: Modern Library, 2001.

[Qur'an] The translation of E. H. Palmer, now in the public domain, for example, at http://sacred-texts.com/isl/sbe06/. Also, *The Qur'an: A New Translation*, by Tarif Khalidi. New York: Penguin, 2009.

[Virgil] *The Aeneid*, translated by Robert Fitzgerald. New York: Vintage Books, 1990. Also, *The Aeneid*, translated by Robert Fagles, introduction by Bernard Knox. New York: Penguin, 2006.

Secondary Sources

Tens of thousands of books and articles could be listed here, and that's counting only the ones published since the beginning of the twentieth century. Those listed here are books that I carefully consulted on several occasions. Others are referenced in the Notes section.

Alter, Robert, and Frank Kermode (eds.). *The Literary Guide to the Bible*. Cambridge: Belknap/Harvard University Press, 1987.

Armstrong, Karen. *Islam: A Short History.* New York: Modern Library, 2002.

Auerbach, Erich. *Mimesis: The Representation of Reality in Western Literature,* translated by Willard R. Trask. Princeton, NJ: Princeton University Press, 1968.

Blackburn, Simon. *Plato's Republic: A Biography.* New York: Atlantic Monthly Press, 2006.

Clark-Soles, Jaime. *Death and the Afterlife in the New Testament.* New York: T&T Clark, 2006.

Eco, Umberto. *The Book of Legendary Lands,* translated by Alastair McEwen. New York: Rizzoli, 2013.

Gilson, Etienne. *Dante the Philosopher,* translated by David Moore. London: Sheed & Ward, 1948.

———. *The Spirit of Mediaeval Philosophy: The Gifford Lectures of 1931–2,* translated by A. H. C. Downes. London: Sheed & Ward, 1950.

Givens, Teryl L. *When Souls Had Wings: Pre-mortal Existence in Western Thought.* New York: Oxford University Press, 2012.

Hawkins, Peter S. *Dante's Testaments: Essays in Scriptural Imagination.* Stanford, CA: Stanford University Press, 1999.

Hughes, Robert. *Rome: A Cultural, Visual, and Personal History.* New York: Vintage Books, 2012.

Kerenyi, Karoly. *The Religion of the Greeks and Romans,* translated by Christopher Holme. London: Thames and Hudson, 1962.

Klonsky, Milton. *Blake's Dante: The Complete Illustrations to the Divine Comedy*; New York: Harmony Books, 1980.

Manuel, Alberto. *Homer's* The Iliad *and* The Odyssey: *A Biography.* New York: Atlantic Monthly Press, 2007.

March, Jenny. *Cassell Dictionary of Classical Mythology.* London: Cassell, 1999.

Mikalson, Jon D. *Ancient Greek Religion.* Malden, MA: Blackwell, 2005.

Russell, Jeffrey Burton. *The Devil: Perceptions of Evil from Antiquity to Primitive Christianity.* Ithaca, NY: Cornell University Press, 1987.

Sayers, Dorothy L., *Introductory Papers on Dante*. New York: Harper & Brothers, 1954.

————. *Further Papers on Dante*. New York: Harper & Brothers, 1957.

Turner, Alice K. *The History of Hell*. New York: Harcourt Brace/Harvest, 1995.

Turner, Denys. *Thomas Aquinas: A Portrait*. New Haven, CT: Yale University Press, 2013.

Williams, Charles. *The Figure of Beatrice: A Study in Dante*. London: Faber and Faber, 1943.

Wilson, A. N. *Dante in Love*. New York: Farrar, Straus and Giroux, 2011.

Winter, Tim (ed.). *The Cambridge Companion to Classical Islamic Theology*. New York: Cambridge University Press, 2008.

About the Author

Jon M. Sweeney is an independent scholar, culture critic, and popular speaker with twenty-five years of experience in spirituality trade publishing. For many years, he was the vice president of marketing for Jewish Lights Publishing and cofounder of SkyLight Paths Publishing, a multifaith trade book publisher in Vermont. Since 2004, he has been editor in chief at Paraclete Press in Massachusetts, where he now serves as publisher. Jon is the author or editor of more than twenty books focusing on popular medieval history and spiritual memoir, including *The Pope Who Quit: A True Medieval Tale of Mystery, Death, and Salvation*, a History Book Club selection that was recently optioned by HBO, Inc.; and *Francis of Assisi in His Own Words: The Essential Writings*. Raised an evangelical Protestant, Jon joined the Catholic Church on the feast day of Saint Francis of Assisi in 2009.